# SELECTIONS FROM THE POETICAL LITERATURE OF THE WEST

SELECTIONS

FROM THE

POETICAL LITERATURE

OF

THE WEST
(1841)

EDITED BY

WILLIAM D. GALLAGHER

A FACSIMILE REPRODUCTION

WITH AN INTRODUCTION

BY

JOHN T. FLANAGAN

GAINESVILLE, FLORIDA

SCHOLARS' FACSIMILES & REPRINTS

1968

SCHOLARS' FACSIMILES & REPRINTS
1605 N.W. 14TH AVENUE
GAINESVILLE, FLORIDA, 32601, U.S.A.

HARRY R. WARFEL, GENERAL EDITOR

REPRODUCED FROM A COPY OWNED BY

JOHN T. FLANAGAN

L.C. CATALOG CARD NUMBER: 68-2 9083

MANUFACTURED IN THE U.S.A.

INTRODUCTION

On April 8, 1850, in Cincinnati, William D. Gallagher delivered the presidential address before the Historical and Philosophical Society of Ohio. Speaking on the general topic of progress in the Northwest, he described the immense land area reaching from western Pennsylvania to the Mississippi River, commented on the climate and natural resources of the region, and traced the influx of settlers who had made possible the formation of seven states of the Union between 1802 and 1850. But he was of course chiefly interested in the future. Comparing his own region to the densely populated countries of northern Europe, he predicted that the Northwest could sustain a population of 126,000,000 though he did not propose a time limit for this explosion of settlement. And he was enthusiastic about the possibilities of a land in which Christianity was dominant and the representative principle in government firmly established. Gallagher asserted: "We have found the extent and character of territory required; we have found the food and clothing; we have found the materials and the means of manufacture, the channels of trade, the climatic influences; we have found all that the physical wants of man can require; and finally, *we have found the men.*"[1]

This affirmation of confidence in the material and cultural potentialities of the Northwest, which came as a kind of climax to Gallagher's editorial and promotional work, places him squarely in the company of James Hall, Timothy Flint, and Dr. Daniel Drake, his Cincinnati contemporaries who

---

[1] *Facts and Conditions of Progress in the North-West* (Cincinnati, 1850), p. 46.

warmly espoused the future of what they liked to call the western country. All of them were sanguine and determined, all of them were a little chauvinistic, and all expressed their convictions in speeches, articles, and books. As a poet, essayist, and editor of several influential periodicals, Gallagher was a significant figure. In the words of William Henry Venable, who knew all of the Cincinnati literati and who wrote an invaluable account of cultural life in the Ohio Valley, "No other man has done so much for the cause of western periodical literature as William D. Gallagher."[2]

I

William Davis Gallagher was born in Philadelphia, August 21, 1808, the son of an Irish refugee. After his father's early death, his widowed mother took her young family in 1816 to Mount Pleasant in Hamilton County, Ohio, and there the boy received his schooling. He attended a Lancastrian seminary and in nearby Cincinnati learned typesetting and proofreading, skills which he relied on for the next dozen years when he was connected with various Ohio periodicals. As early as 1826 Gallagher worked on an agricultural paper called *The Western Tiller*. Subsequently he was employed by the *Cincinnati Register*, the *Western Minerva*, and the *Xenia Backwoodsman*, a political organ devoted to the presidential campaign of Henry Clay. All of these periodicals were short-lived and unremunerative. For a brief period he was associated with the *Ohio State Journal* at Columbus, and from 1839 to 1850 he acted as associate editor under Charles Hammond and subsequently as editor of the *Cincinnati Gazette*. But before he accepted this position he had attempted to edit his own literary journal, the *Hesperian*, in 1838 and 1839. Assisted by Otway Curry, he managed to issue three volumes of this monthly in Columbus and Cincinnati but had to desist because of lack of financial support.

---

[2] W. H. Venable, *Beginnings of Literary Culture in the Ohio Valley* (Cincinnati, 1891), p. 80.

INTRODUCTION   vii

It was during his editorship of the *Hesperian* that Gallagher made his most important contributions to the cultural development of the region. Timothy Flint and James Hall had preceded him as editors of literary periodicals in Cincinnati, and Moncure Conway was to attempt an Ohio Valley *Dial* in 1860. Despite the herculean efforts of the editors to support their journals by their own pens, all succumbed after a brief existence. The *Hesperian* was no exception; yet during its short life it was read and appreciated. The editor sought material on such indigenous topics as the Indian mounds of the Ohio Valley, early French settlements, internal trade, mineral and vegetable deposits, agricultural resources, and river steamboats. Like most western magazines it was overly factual and employed a good deal of borrowed material; the periodicals of the Atlantic seaboard were ruthlessly levied on. Yet many writers from the Cincinnati area contributed to the *Hesperian*—Benjamin Drake, James H. Perkins, and James Freeman Clarke for example—and Gallagher was justly proud of its western note. The editor himself provided editorials and criticism, as well as his longest piece of prose fiction, "The Dutchman's Daughter," which ran serially through the third volume but was never collected in book form.

A few years after the demise of the *Hesperian*, Gallagher contributed a review of western periodical literature to another magazine in which he defended his venture with some acerbity. As editor he claimed that he had secured the best talent available in the West and that the magazine had been received with acclaim. Blunders in the business office as much as anything else, he declared, were responsible for its discontinuance after only eighteen months. His personal stake in the *Hesperian* had been high, and he was understandably annoyed when the journal failed. As he observed: "This work was so exclusively one of the writer's own projection; it was made to bend so entirely to his ideas of what such a periodical should be; his own pen furnished so large a proportion of its entire contents; his reputation was so intimately connected with it; his fame and fortune so staked upon its success, and his humiliation at its failure so deep and abiding, that he feels he is not the proper one to write its history."[3] The *Hesperian* represented high editorial standards and an attractive diversification of subject matter. Despite its basically literary orientation its pages contained scientific, historical, and philosophical material. It was one of the half-dozen best magazines to appear in the trans-Allegheny region in the mid-century.

In 1850 Gallagher temporarily gave up journalism to become private secretary to Thomas Corwin, the Secretary of the Treasury: after two years in Washington he bought a part interest in and became editor of the *Louisville Daily Courier*, establishing his home in Pewee Valley, Oldham County, Kentucky. From 1854 to 1860 he edited the *Western Farmer's Journal* from his Kentucky residence. Gallagher was a delegate to the Republican National Convention in 1860 and supported Lincoln. The next year he was appointed private secretary to Salmon P. Chase, Secretary of the Treasury in Lincoln's cabinet. During the Civil War he was named a special collector of customs and commercial agent in the upper Mississippi Valley and later still surveyor of the customs and pension agent in Louisville. These political activities demanded most of his energy, and he wrote nothing of consequence in his closing years. He died June 27, 1894.[4]

---

[3] W. D. Gallagher, "Periodical Literature," *Western Literary Journal and Monthly Review*, November, 1844, Vol. I, p. 5.

[4] There are two brief but accurate accounts of Gallagher's life: by Douglass W. Miller in the *Dictionary of American Biography* (New York, 1931), Vol. VII, pp. 102-3; and by Tom Burns Haber in *Ohio Authors and Their Books*, ed. William Coyle (Cleveland and New York, 1962), pp. 232-233. Venable in the previously cited work gives a more diffuse and personal account (chapter fifteen).

II.

Whatever literary reputation Gallagher enjoys today must be based on his poetry. As a young man he began to write and publish verse, and as a septuagenarian he was still collecting and presumably adding to his achievement. Much of his verse remains scattered through the magazines which blossomed almost everywhere in the Ohio Valley and soon wilted. Equally ephemeral were the ballads or songs which once attracted enough attention to be sung from the platforms of music halls. His romantic Indian lyric, "The Spotted Fawn," was made popular by a vocalist named Duffield in 1845 and became widely known. But Gallagher did not see fit to include it in his collected poems of 1881.[5]

In the spring of 1835 Gallagher published a booklet of thirty-six pages entitled *Erato, No. I*; in September of the same year it was succeeded by *Erato, No. II*, with sixty pages. A third collection, *Erato, No. III*, appeared in 1837. Today these thin gatherings are rare items. Some of this early verse Gallagher chose to include in his *Selections from the Poetical Literature of the West*, which the U. P. James firm of Cincinnati published for him in 1841. It is interesting to note that the anthology opens with a selection from "Miami Woods," Gallagher's most sustained poem, and a blank verse work which led the writer of the biographical sketch in the *Dictionary of American Biography* to remark that Gallagher had done for the charm of the Ohio forests what Bryant had done for the woodlands of New England. Gallagher continued to work on "Miami Woods" throughout the next decades and in 1881 made it the initial poem of his most substantial volume *Miami Woods, A Golden Wedding and Other Poems,* published by Robert Clarke & Company of Cincinnati. In its final form the poem has seven parts as

---

[5] The text is printed in William T. Coggeshall, *The Poets and Poetry of the West* (Columbus, 1860), p. 144. Coggeshall also includes a well known parody of the poem.

well as a proem and a l'envoy, and the appended dates suggest that the composition of the work spanned at least twenty years.

A previously unpublished letter from Gallagher to Lewis J. Cist, a Cincinnati banker and poet, confirms the carelessness that authors often show concerning their own work and the later difficulties experienced when they try to collect it. Gallagher wrote as follows:

Louisville 5-11-81

My dear Cist:

Now that you are no longer playing Night Hawk for the Post-office, perhaps you can find time to do a little job for me. You may remember that between 45 and 50 years ago—(just think of it: nearly half a century! You must be getting quite old)—I published three small, thin volumes of poems, entitled *"Erato."* In these little books (if *books* they may be called) are a number of pieces which I wish to include in the "Collection" that I am making—or, rather, trying to make. I haven't a copy of either of them. Will you not do me the favor to inquire among old friends of yours and old friends of mine in Cincinnati, for the purpose of "lighting upon" a copy of "The Last Appeal," which I *think* appeared in the first number of the series. But there are a dozen other poems, I presume, in the three numbers, which I ought to have. "I tell you"—and you may "bet" the first nickle you find—that if I ever get to be a youngster again, I'll take at least *some sort* of care of the bantlings of my brains, be they "good, bad, or indifferent."

I think it possible that you may find copies

of the second and third "Erato" at the bookstore of my old friend U. P. James: but the *first* number, I very much fear, will be sought for in vain. The leading Poem in that was "The Penitent;" but what the miscellaneous poems were, with the exception of "The Last Appeal," I have not the slightest idea.

I hope you are still looking into the Past, and photographing its footsteps, for the entertainment of the Present.

Truly yours,

W. H. GALLAGHER[6]

It is interesting to note that four of the fourteen poems which Gallagher included in his *Selections from the Poetical Literature of the West* do not reappear in the 1881 volume and that he finally excluded both "The Penitent" and "The Last Appeal," mentioned in the preceding letter, from the final collection. His preface to *Miami Woods, A Golden Wedding and Other Poems* promises the reader that a subsequent volume will include other verse, notably border ballads and miscellaneous poems of later years, but this publication did not materialize. Thus, although a good deal of Gallagher's verse remains scattered through various fugitive periodicals, his only accessible volume contains some forty-seven brief lyrics and the more ambitious descriptive poem, "Miami Woods."

Most of his poetry is admittedly undistinguished. Despite a limited education he early mastered the technique of verse and showed a command of prosody from his first published lines. He used many forms: stanzas of varying length,

---

[6] Letter in the possession of John T. Flanagan. It was written on the letterhead of the Kentucky Land Company with offices in Chicago and Louisville. Gallagher was listed as secretary.

quatrains, couplets, blank verse, ballads. His rhymes are precise if not specially original and his lines have a melody which often becomes banal. His diction is conventional; certainly he rarely freed himself from romantic cliches. This imitative quality was unfortunately compounded by his tendency to choose obvious and familiar themes: motherhood, the charms of spring, autumn's fullness, duty, and a nostalgia for departed youth. Only rarely did he escape from the constrictions of such topics and seldom did he speak in a more individual voice.

But there are exceptions. A poem called "Conservatism" contrasts the owl and the eagle to the detriment of the bird of night. Its first stanza is effective in its simplicity.

> The Owl, he fareth well
> In the shadows of the night;
> And it puzzleth him to tell
> Why the Eagle loves the light.[7]

After some exposition of the respective functions of the birds, the poem closes with the owl returning to his abode of darkness and the eagle sweeping away on its strong, bold pinions. Gallagher extolled dandelions—"Bright horologe of seasons"—in a poem which does not suffer by comparison with Lowell's on the same subject. He praised the cardinal in a tribute full of references, not to the eglantine and the lark as elsewhere, but to May-apples, Solomon's seal, anemones, crab apples, and tulip trees—all characteristic of the Ohio Valley which he knew so well.

Generally orthodox in his own opinions except for a strong anti-slavery bias and a firm belief in the dignity of manual toil, Gallagher usually celebrated the obvious platitudes, morality, duty, industry, humility, but sometimes in memorable lines. No better example of this can be found than the

---

[7] *Miami Woods, A Golden Wedding and Other Poems* (Cincinnati, 1881), p. 183.

poem "Truth and Freedom," which encourages principled action and the courage to suffer if necessary. The closing two stanzas justify quotation:

> Be thou like the first apostles—
> Be thou like heroic Paul:
> If a free thought seek expression,
> Speak it boldly! speak it all!
>
> Face thine enemies—accusers;
> Scorn the prison, rack, or rod!
> And, if thou hast TRUTH to utter,
> *Speak*! and leave the rest to God.[8]

As a boy living in the country on the outskirts of Cincinnati, Gallagher had the usual rural experiences, roaming through the woods, gathering nuts and berries, watching or hunting small animals and birds, growing gradually more conscious of the mysteries of the changing seasons. Despite years of urban residence this passion for the world of nature never left him, and he retained his fondness for strolling through the glades and woods of southern Ohio. Like Wordsworth, the rural scenes brought him therapy and a deep philosophical content. Gallagher's devotion to the out-of-doors and his awareness of the protean moods and colors of the forest help to make "Miami Woods" his most impressive piece of work.

The poem is primarily descriptive and gains what coherence it has from the personality of the poet. Two themes are prominent. In a mood of nostalgia he remembers the delights of boyhood when, in the words of another bard, "the thoughts of youth are long, long thoughts." Although maturity and domestic cares have separated him from the scenes of early delight, he recalls the airiness of the woods and the special hues of spring and fall, and as an older man

---

[8] *Ibid.*, p. 182.

he returns periodically for solitary rambles along familiar paths. Certain scenes also remind him of personal grief, and he alludes to the burial of his children in infancy. In particular the poem assumes the tone of the elegy as the poet expresses his sorrow over the loss of a beloved daughter. But Gallagher characteristically preserves his abiding faith in providence; his reverence for the Maker of the universe remains unshaken. The world of nature, of which the Miami woods were the enduring symbol, is for him always the creation of a superior power but never divinity itself. There is none of Bryant's pantheistic creed in Gallagher's poem, although at times the lines of "Miami Woods" suggest the older poet.

Gallagher never wrote more mellifluously than in this his longest poem. Occasional lyrics or brief odes interrupt the blank verse, but generally the unrhymed lines march on with dignity, smoothness, and ease. The descriptions of seasonal changes are particularly effective. Thoroughly consistent in his conviction that a western writer should write of the region he knew best, Gallagher introduced indigenous trees and plants into his lines rather than settling for the stereotypes of English romanticism. Autumn burst upon his eye with a blaze of glory.

> Here, where the poplar rears its yellow crest,
> A golden glory; yonder, where the oak
> Stands monarch of the forest, and the ash
> Is girt with flame-like parasite, and broad
> The dogwood spreads beneath, and, fringing all,
> The sumac blushes to the ground, a flood
> Of deepest crimson; and afar, where looms
> The gnarled gum, a cloud of bloodiest red.[9]

---

[9] *Ibid.*, pp. 15-16. Gallagher apparently revised this poem: in the passage quoted the poplar replaces the maple, and a line about the sumac has been added.

Under such cover live the partridge, the wild turkey, and even in Gallagher's day the wild pigeon, all feeding on the abundant mast of the forest. Grapes and persimmons, in addition to various kinds of nuts, lure the wild creatures to the woods, where the poet could not only enjoy their sparkle and cries but could also hear the "solemn Anthem of the Centuries." In a different season the forest floor produced violets and anemones, briar roses and dogwood buds, while the "bent catalpa waves its fan-like leaves / And lifts its milk-white blossoms." This perennial charm of the forest did not dim with the poet's increasing years, for in the second part of the work he could write:

> The groves, whose beauty and whose music stole
> Into my wondering spirit long ago,
> Were ne'er more beautiful than now, were ne'er
> More musical.[10]

Other aspects of the western scene also intrigued Gallagher. He devoted several vivid lines to the tumuli, the burial mounds, and even the geometrical designs left by a more ancient people than the lingering aborigines whom the poet might have known.

In the fifth part of the poem the coming of Indian summer with its belated warmth and opulent color made him think of the red men who gave their name to the most delightful of American seasons. But his recollections were both pacific and troubled. He could speak approvingly of such symbols of the pioneer backwoodsmen as Boone and Kenton; he could also refer to Pontiac, and to the broken-hearted chief Logan, and to war leaders like Tecumseh and the Prophet, while the massacre at the River Raisin, an event of his childhood, was still in his memory. But when Indian summer was terminated with the arrival of winds from Lake

---

[10] *Ibid.*, p. 37.

Huron and the straits of Mackinac, the poet faced with resignation the onslaught of winter.

Woven alternately through the poem with specific descriptions of nature and allusions to earlier inhabitants of the West are celebrations of the abstractions which always please the conventional poet, celebrations of duty, morality, peace, happiness, beauty. In "Miami Woods" Gallagher paid tribute to order and freedom, which together he conceived to be God's highest gift, his primordial law. He eschewed the mock freedom extolled by the Greek orators who praised liberty and ignored the slavery and wretchedness around them, and he disdained the ersatz order in western Europe which crumbled before a wave of nationalist revolutions. With more than a touch of chauvinism he proclaimed America as the hope of freedom and the scene of an order derived from God. Only across the western ocean, "where the adventurous Genoese descried / Another world" was the ideal to be found.

III.

It must be admitted that the importance of Gallagher's anthology, *Selections from the Poetical Literature of the West*, published at Cincinnati in 1841, is primarily historical. The first collection ever made of the verse written by Ohio Valley poets, it is less remarkable for its high literary quality than as evidence of the amount and variety of poetry being written in the West in the first decades of the nineteenth century. Few volumes of verse were published beyond the Alleghenies at that time, though it is true that in addition to occasional books issued by Cincinnati publishers, Angus Umphraville published his *Missourian Lays, and Other Western Ditties* in St. Louis in 1821, and Horatio Cooke his *Gleanings of Thought* in Chicago in 1843.

But the absence of many *volumes* of verse does not imply that poetry was not being written and published. Indeed, the many literary magazines, with some of which

INTRODUCTION xvii

Gallagher himself was associated, encouraged poetasters of all types and welcomed metrical contributions. The last page of each issue of the *Cincinnati Literary Gazette,* which John P. Foote edited in 1824 and 1825, was frequently devoted to verse, a fact which may startle the modern reader who is accustomed to finding poetry only as filler material for magazines. Indeed the editor once observed that he would welcome literary and scientific material because a plethora of verse threatened to crowd his pages. "Poetry is in so flourishing a state on our side of the river, that the limits allotted to that department are preoccupied."[11] Thus if few poets had the means to collect their work in substantial books, many could appear in print in the most reputable literary magazines—and a little later in the annuals—of the day.

In the introduction to his anthology Gallagher rightly pointed to the non-professional character of his contributors. They were poets by avocation, poets in spare moments stolen from other activities, "some amid the din of the workshop, others at the handle of the plough, a third class in the ledger-marked counting-room, and a fourth among the John-Doism and Richard-Roism of an attorney's office." They wrote when the mood seized them and opportunity arose— lawyers, physicians, engineers, clergymen, teachers, housewives. The major point is that they wrote at all and that when they wrote they expressed themselves in meter by preference.

Since Gallagher did not see fit to identify his contributors, a few biographical facts seem pertinent. James Hall, although represented by only one poem in the anthology, was probably the best known. A versatile man who was an attorney, banker, and editor, he is more famous today for his short stories about the West and for his statistical books about the economic history of the region than for his poetry, but he contributed a substantial amount of verse to such

---

[11] Editorial, *Cincinnati Literary Gazette,* February 21, 1824, Vol. I.

annuals as *The Western Souvenir* and to magazines. Otway Curry was Gallagher's associate editor on the *Hesperian* and a minor literary figure in Cincinnati. Micah Flint, the son of Timothy Flint, contributed verse to several periodicals and published in 1826 a volume entitled *The Hunter, and Other Poems.* James Freeman Clarke, the Unitarian editor of *The Western Messenger* at Louisville, was subsequently a pastor in Boston and an associate of the Concord transcendentalists. Albert Pike, a New Englander who went to the Southwest, became notable as a lawyer and journalist, served in the Mexican War, and became a general in the Confederate Army. Frederick Thomas was a novelist and essayist who was also the author of a long poem called *The Emigrant*, 1833. Thomas Shreve was a coeditor of the *Cincinnati Mirror* with Gallagher and later a Louisville businessman. Charles A. Jones contributed satiric poetry to the *Cincinnati Gazette* and later practised law; he was the author of a volume called *The Outlaw, and Other Poems*, 1835. James H. Perkins, a versatile writer of both prose and verse, contributed to magazines edited by both Hall and Gallagher and compiled the still useful *Annals of the West* in 1846.

Of the feminine contributors to the anthology, Mrs. Caroline Lee Hentz was best known; she wrote a number of popular novels and was also a minor playwright. Mrs. Amelia B. Welby was a sentimental poet who spent much of her life in Louisville. Mrs. Anna P. Dinnies was a resident of St. Louis who had earlier contributed frequently to Hall's *Illinois Monthly Magazine* under the pseudonym of "Moina." Mrs. Rebecca S. Nichols also used a nom de plume, "Kate Cleaveland," published verse in several eastern periodicals, and for a time edited a Cincinnati literary magazine. Mrs. Julia L. Dumont, a schoolteacher in Vevay, Indiana, is perhaps remembered best as the instructor of the youthful Edward Eggleston.

These figures, and some others even more obscure today, make up the thirty-seven poets plus the editor who are represented in Gallagher's anthology. Their subjects are expectedly conventional for the most part: love, beauty, patriotism, death, happiness, and the world of nature. Only a few were significantly conscious of their western background despite the editor's insistence that they all had close links with the West. The Indian mounds or tumuli which dotted the Ohio Valley excited the fancies of several. Tecumseh attracted one poet, western scenery either served as the actual subject or provided important local color for a few lyrics, and there were odes to or celebrations of geographical landmarks such as Lake Erie, the Ohio River, and even the Rocky Mountains—although here the place was only a device for the writer to express his feeling of change and desertion. Most of the poetry is deadly serious and in a now faded romantic tradition, though it could not have seemed so to readers in the 1840's. Any touch of irony or comedy, as the closing lines of James W. Ward's "The Musquetoe's Song" suggest, was certainly unintentional.[12]

It is well to note that nineteen years after Gallagher's pioneer western anthology had appeared, William T. Coggeshall, like his predecessor an Ohio journalist and editor, published a similar volume, *The Poets and Poetry of the West*. Coggeshall's anthology is a much bulkier book and includes the work of some 159 poets; moreover, he included extensive biographical notices. Despite a more extensive representation which was obviously based on a much larger body of available verse, Coggeshall like Gallagher insisted on the non-professional character of his contributors: "The poets of the West are, or have been, lawyers, doctors, teachers,

---

[12] Evert A. Duyckinck and George L. Duyckinck in their *Cyclopaedia of American Literature* (New York, 1856), Vol. II, p. 471, praised Gallagher's work: "In 1841 Mr. Gallagher edited a volume entitled *Selections from the Poetical Literature of the West*, a work peculiarly appropriate for one who had done so much by his labors in behalf of literature, as well as his own contributions to the common stock, to foster and honor the necessarily arduous pursuit of literature in a new country."

preachers, mechanics, farmers, editors, printers, and housekeepers."[13] Among the new contributors were the Cary sisters, John James Piatt, Sarah T. Bolton, the younger brother of William Cullen Bryant, John Bryant, and William Dean Howells. But no single poet was given as much space as Gallagher, twenty-one of whose poems appear in the collection. Indeed, Coggeshall praised Gallagher for his graphic power and for the humanitarian quality of his later writing.[14] It is apparent that Coggeshall's aim like Gallagher's was to represent as many poetic voices in the West as possible.

The reader of both these anthologies will quickly conclude that no major poet had appeared in the Ohio Valley before 1860. The literary genius of the region was more conspicuously present in the prose—the fiction, the biography and autobiography, the essays, the reviews, the history which largely sustained the innumerable magazines of the age. Writers like Schoolcraft, Hall, Flint, Eggleston, Daniel and Benjamin Drake, Joseph and Matthew Field of St. Louis, not to mention Mark Twain later on, were primarily writers of prose, either imaginative or factual. But the two anthologies of western verse are revealing examples of what the minor poets were doing, and Gallagher's *Selections* especially emphasizes the fact that literate if not strikingly original writing existed and even found an audience in the Middle West well before the Civil War.[15]

JOHN T. FLANAGAN

Urbana, Illinois
February 10, 1968.

---

[13] Coggeshall, *The Poets and Poetry of the West*, p. vi.
[14] Coggeshall, p. 136.
[15] In 1909 Emerson Venable compiled an anthology limited to the poets of the Buckeye State, *Poets of Ohio* (Cincinnati, 1909). Gallagher is the first poet to appear in the collection, and the seventeen poems allotted to him include extracts from "Miami Woods" and seven shorter poems.

WESTERN POETRY

SELECTIONS

FROM THE

POETICAL LITERATURE

OF

THE WEST.

"Here is a wreath,
With many an unripe blossom garlanded,
And many a weed, yet mingled with some flowers
Which will not wither."

CINCINNATI:
PUBLISHED BY U. P. JAMES,
NO. 26 PEARL STREET.
::::::
1841.

Entered according to the act of Congress, in the year 1841, by U. P. JAMES, in the Clerk's office of the District Court of the United States, in and for the District of Ohio.

R. P. BROOKS, PRINTER.

PREFACE.

A VOLUME made up exclusively of the POETICAL LITERATURE OF THE WEST, will perhaps be received with a dubious shake of the head, by many worthy persons, and a wonder whether any good thing *can* come out of *that* Nazareth. And when it is found that such volume contains selections from about two score of writers,—all poets, of course, and *western* poets, too!—the wonder will perhaps be changed into downright amazement at the vanity of our pretensions, and the doubt become absolute incredulity as to any merit therein. Well—this must be even so. It is the tax which our present aim to show what we are, and what we have been, will have to pay upon our past modesty.

Hitherto, for the most part, we have been content to cast our pearls about with a careless hand, often without any mark by which their true ownership could in a disputed case be established, and nearly always regardless as to what might be their future fate. The consequence of this piece of folly is, that now, when we see the value that is set upon such things in other quarters of the earth, and with true world-wisdom seek to reap our harvest with the rest, we are utterly astonished, ourselves, at the extent of our past prodigality.

To correct an error which, judging from numerous recent demonstrations, is one of no inconsiderable magnitude, is certainly worth an effort; and it is for the purpose of making such correction, that the present volume, rendered the more necessary by the apparently studied determination of our Atlantic neighbors to do nothing which will have a tendency to bring us into competition with them, has been compiled. That all concerned would be quite as well off, were some portions of its contents permitted to continue the quiet vagabond existence which they have till now led, hardly admits of a doubt. Other portions, however, are believed to be well deserving of the mark of respect which is here shown them. But in thus provoking examination of the merits of these latter, there is no intention, how well soever it may be thought they will pass an ordeal which has lately sanctified much that was not before esteemed particularly worthy of regeneration, of holding them up as in any manner faultless.

With reference to the design and character of the volume, a word or two, somewhat more in soberness than the preceding, may be proper. The original plan contemplated a collection of the poetical productions of some five or six western writers, whose efforts in this department of literature are generally regarded as having been more successful than those of the large majority who have here attempted to "build the lofty rhyme." Upon this plan, a considerable part of the volume was prepared; but being struck, in the prosecution of it, with the equal merit and fitness of productions which it did not embrace, the compiler was induced to double the number of writers to be selected from; and subsequently yielding to other suggestions, he changed almost entirely the original design, and made the collection as general as the materials in his possession, or readily accessible, permitted.

There was still no effort, however, to present in its pages, samples of the verse of *all* who have, with more or less success, attempted poetry in this region. This would have been a departure from the original plan so wide as to have destroyed, wholly, the object first had in view. It would, moreover, have trenched upon the grounds of another, much better qualified for such a task than the writer of this, who has been engaged for years, at intervals of leisure, in collecting materials for a work of that kind. This explanation is given for the information of those who, with real claims to consideration in a volume professing to embrace a *complete* list of our writers in the department of literature under view, might otherwise think themselves carelessly overlooked, or designedly slighted, in the preparation of this. This volume is not sent forth, as by any means *the whole* of the " Poetical Literature of the West." It is believed, however, that it will represent its character pretty faithfully, as it certainly contains samples of its greatest excellences, its mediocre qualities, and its worst defects.

Much the greater number of the persons selected from, are either western born or western educated, or both; and all of them who are now living, with a single exception, are citizens of this section of the Union. The exception referred to, is that of a young clergyman, whose feeble health, after a residence here of five or six years, compelled him, much against his inclination, to abandon a field in which he had hoped to labor for life. His poetical tendencies, it is believed, received their first considerable impetus here. His fancy delighted to plunge into the depths of our interminable forests, and to skim the clear surface of our beautiful rivers and lakes. And these, more than any thing else, were the inspiration of his muse. His productions breathe of them in every line, and are well worthy of preservation; and as they are not likely to be collected into any other volume, there seems to be a manifest propriety in inserting them in this, although we cannot claim their esteemed author, as a western man or a western writer.

Selections will be found in the volume from one individual, who is western only in character and by adoption, and who had " written for posterity" before his eye caught, from the summits of the Alleghanies, its first glimpse of that glorious region, which his heart at once told him was to be his home henceforth forever. Choice has been made, how-

PREFACE.

ever, only from what he has written since that period, under the inspiration of new scenes, and in what was to him, to no small extent, a new state of society.

Of the productions generally, which make up the volume, this remark may be made: they look not, for their paternity, to men of either leisure, wealth, or devotion to letters,—but find it, some amid the din of the workshop, others at the handle of the plough, a third class in the ledger-marked counting-room, and a fourth among the John-Doism and Richard-Roism of an attorney's office. For the most part, they have been the mere momentary outgushings of irrepressible feeling, proceeding from the hearts of those who were daily and hourly subjected to the perplexities and toils of business, and the cares and anxieties inseparable from the procuring of one's daily bread by active occupation.—As such, let them be judged.

W. D. G.

CINCINNATI, FEBRUARY, 1841.

CONTENTS.

WILLIAM D. GALLAGHER.

	Page
Miami Woods,	13
The Mothers of the West,	53
Our Early Days,	65
Spring Verses,	73
May,	93
A Rhyme of May Morning,	107
The Mountain Paths,	124
A Summer Scene,	137
August,	146
Harvest Hymn,	157
Lines to a Poetess,	177
Happiness: a Picture,	204
The Laborer,	239
Olden Memories,	263

JOHN M. HARNEY.

Lines on a valued friend,	20
The Fever Dream,	61

JOHN B. DILLON.

The Prophet's Dream,	21
Burial of the Beautiful,	117

GEORGE D. PRENTICE.

The Closing Year,	24
New-England,	188
The Flight of Years,	206
Birth-day of Washington,	257

FREDERICK W. THOMAS.

Impromptu,	27
"Extract from the Emigrant,"	43
Stanzas,	155
War song of '76,	193
"'T is said that Absence conquers Love,"	259

CONTENTS.

Page.
NATHANIEL WRIGHT.
The Mountain Storm, ... 28

JAMES HALL.
Wedded Love's First Home, ... 32

OTWAY CURRY.
The goings forth of God, ... 34
The Minstrel's Home, ... 68
Pauline to the Portrait of Napoleon, ... 108
Satan, ... 141
The Armies of the Eve, ... 154
Autumn Musings, ... 160
Lines of the Life to Come, ... 182
To a Midnight Phantom, ... 236

THOMAS H. SHREVE.
To a Poetess, ... 36
Midnight Musings, ... 70
Youth's Vision of the Future, ... 112
To an Indian Mound, ... 191
The Bliss of Home, ... 221

JAMES H. PERKINS.
Tasso—in Prison, ... 38
Spiritual Presence, ... 74
To a Child, ... 110
The Young Soldier, ... 152
To a Lady, ... 184
Of one now Far Away, ... 198
A Hymn, ... 214
Arnold of Wilkenreid, ... 244
Song, ... 262

CHARLES A. JONES.
Tecumseh, ... 40
The Old Mound, ... 76
The Clouds, ... 121
The Pioneers, ... 186

CHARLES D. DRAKE.
Love's Constancy, ... 45
Life, ... 169

GEORGE B. WALLIS.
A Sonnet, ... 46
The Revolutioners, ... 78
My Locust Tree, ... 127

CONTENTS.

ALBERT PIKE.
To the Mocking Bird, ... 47
Lines written upon the Rocky Mountains, . . . 164

MICAH P. FLINT.
On passing the Grave of a Sister, ... 50
After a Storm, ... 145

MRS. AMELIA B. WELBY.
The Sleeping Infant, ... 55
My Sisters, ... 104
The Freed Bird, ... 115
"When shines the Star," 143
"I know that thy Spirit," 158
To a Sea-Shell, ... 166
The Blind Girl, ... 250

MRS. ANNE P. DINNIES.
The Wife, ... 57
Wedded Love, ... 97

MRS. LAURA M. THURSTON.
On crossing the Alleghanies, ... 59
The Green Hills of my Father Land, ... 101
The Paths of Life, ... 221

MRS. SARAH J. HOWE.
The Egyptian Girl's song, ... 83

EPHRAIM PEABODY.
Falls of a Forest Stream, ... 82
The Ohio, ... 119
Lake Erie, ... 172
The Backwoodsman, ... 195
Western Scenery, ... 217

WILLIAM WALLACE.
Jerusalem, ... 86
To the Star Lyra, ... 211

JAMES F. CLARKE.
The Violet, ... 88
Jacob's Well, ... 203
To a Bunch of Flowers, ... 230

JAMES W. WARD.
The Musquetoe's Song, ... 90

CONTENTS.

JAMES B. MARSHALL.
	Page.
Lines to Mary,	92
To Eva: in her Album,	173

MRS. REBECCA S. NICHOLS.
Musings,	99

HARVEY D. LITTLE.
"On Judah's Hills,"	129
Palmyra,	150
The Wanderer's Return,	175

LEWIS RINGE.
The Kanhawa,	130

LEWIS J. CIST.
"My Beautiful—My Own."	132

EDWIN R. CAMPBELL.
"Let there be Light,"	142

LEWIS F. THOMAS.
Lines to a Lady,	149
To Ione,	180

WILLIAM B. FAIRCHILD.
Childhood,	178

HUGH PETERS.
My Native Land,	200
Connecticut: A Fragment,	223
The Parting,	234

MRS. JULIA L. DUMONT.
The Tumulus,	219

MRS. CAROLINE LEE HENTZ.
Epilogue,	226

G. G. FOSTER.
Ode to the Press,	232

PEYTON S. SYMMES.
Lines on Greece,	241

WILLIAM NEWTON.
History,	253

JAMES G. DRAKE.
Parlez Bas,	260

SELECT POEMS.

MIAMI WOODS.

BY WILLIAM D. GALLAGHER.

The Autumn Time is with us!—Its approach
Was heralded, not many days ago,
By hazy skies, that veil'd the brazen sun,
And sea-like murmurs from the rustling corn,
And low-voiced brooks, that wandered drowsily
By purpling clusters of the juicy grape,
Swinging upon the vine. And now, 'tis here!
And what a change hath pass'd upon the face
Of Nature, where the waving forest spreads,
Then robed in deepest green! All through the night
The subtle frost hath plied its mystic art;
And in the day the golden sun hath wrought
True wonders; and the winds of morn and even
Have touch'd with magic breath the changing leaves.
And now, as wanders the dilating eye
Athwart the varied landscape, circling far,
What gorgeousness, what blazonry, what pomp

Of colors, bursts upon the ravish'd sight!
Here, where the maple rears its yellow crest,
A golden glory: yonder, where the oak
Stands monarch of the forest, and the ash
Is girt with flame-like parasite, and broad
The dogwood spreads beneath, a rolling field
Of deepest crimson; and afar, where looms
The gnarlèd gum, a cloud of bloodiest red!

 Out in the woods of Autumn!—I have cast
Aside the shackles of the town, that vex
The fetterless soul, and come to hide myself,
Miami! in thy venerable shades.
Low on thy bank, where spreads the velvet moss,
My limbs recline. Beneath me, silver-bright,
Glide the clear waters, with a plaintive moan
For summer's parting glories. High o'erhead,
Seeking the sedgy lakes of the warm South,
Sails tireless the unerring waterfowl,
Screaming among the cloud-racks. Oft from where,
Erect on mossy trunk, the partridge stands,
Bursts suddenly the whistle clear and loud,
Far-echoing through the dim wood's fretted aisles.
Deep murmurs from the trees, bending with brown
And ripened mast, are interrupted now
By sounds of dropping nuts; and warily
The turkey from the thicket comes, and swift
As flies an arrow darts the pheasant down,
To batten on the autumn; and the air,

At times, is darkened by a sudden rush
Of myriad wings, as the wild pigeon leads
His squadrons to the banquet. Far away,
Where the pawpaw its mellow fruitage yields,
And thick, dark clusters of the wild grape hang,
The merry laugh of childhood, and the shout
Of truant schoolboy, ring upon the air.

Deep in the solemn forest!—From the tops
Of these old trees, swept by the evening wind,
Which swells among their leaves, and dies away,
And gathers strength again, float softly down
Strange, wild, deep harmonies. And I have been
All day among the Voices of the Wood,
That are but echoes of perpetual tones
With which God fills the universe. The noon,
Gairish and still, and midnight's calm repose,
And dewy eve, and blue rejoicing morn,
Are full of them. I hear them in the breeze
That stirs the reed to music. In the faint,
Sad murmur of the stream that glides below,
Bearing away the fallen leaves, as pass
The dreams of childhood and the hopes of life,
I hear them. And I hear them in the spring
That, bubbling from beneath yon dark old root,
Falls tinkling o'er the mossy rock below.
And in the billowy chimes that wake aloft
When gale-like breezes sweep the ancient trees,
They speak with organ-tones, that reach the depths

Stirring within me, and an echo find
In the roused soul......O God! Thou art in all
I now behold! the essence and the life,
The germ and the vitality! the birth,
The being, and the end! Else Reason gropes
In darkness all her days, and Knowledge dies.
What but the high intelligence, the hand
Almighty, and the sempiternal life—
What but the omnipresence, and the will,
All which we feel Thou art, and all which fills
Our great Idea of a primal cause
And final end, could speak this glorious world
From wildest Chaos and profoundest Night?
What poise the planets in the void, and set
The infinite stars in order, and confine
Each in its separate path on high? What fill
Earth with its countless forms of Life, and raise
Eternally, as ages glide along,
New being from the ashes of decay?

Alone, with God and Nature!—Round me now
Is pressing onward the eternal change.
And here, where all is seen, but nought reveal'd,
I contemplate the mysteries sublime
Of birth, and life, and death.....From the dark womb
Of winter, comes the spring, with mild, warm breath;
And instantly the chains that bound the streams
Are loosen'd, and the waters leap to light,
And shout with gladness. Soon the spell that long

Has held the earth, is broken; and the grass
Pierces the sod, and from the sheltering leaves
That strew the ground, look out the fresh, young flowers,
Smiling to heaven. Then the gray, leafless trees,
Long desolate in their utter nakedness,
Feel the new presence; and, although no sign
Of life is visible, a delicate green
Creeps out along the tender twigs, where swell
The germ-infolding buds; and in the warm
And sunny day, and through the breezy night,
Come forth the myriad leaves, courting the light
And wantoning with the zephyr, till a robe
Of brightest green bursts on the wondering eye.
O'er the cold bosom of the sluggish clod
Soon steals the influence; and from the broad
And seeded field shoots up the waving grain,
Till spreads a sea of verdure far around,
Toss'd by the winds, and with the clouds at play.
Then comes the long and sunny summer time,
And for the garners of the husbandman
Ripens, and to the sickle lays, the grain;
And for the cherish'd tribes of air, that make
The cool groves vocal, strews the briery glebe
With berries; and for the innumerous flocks
That shun the haunts of men, and hang their nests
High in the endless wood, or in the low
Dark thicket build, matures the beechen mast;
And takes the worm upon the leaf, and wraps
A silken tissue round it; and prepares

For all the insect race befitting tombs,
Where each shall sleep the winter hours away.
Then comes the lone and quiet autumn on,
With tinckling water-falls, and moaning woods,
And arid wastes, o'er which the night-winds sigh.
And this is here; and still the eternal round
Of change goes on—beginning, being, ending;
And still the mystery proclaims a Hand
Omnipotent—an Eye that never sleeps.

End of the vernal year!—The flower hath closed
And cast its petals, and the naked stalk
Stands shrivelling in the frost; the feathered grass
Is heavy in the head; the painted leaf
Flies twittering on the wind; and to the earth
Falls the brown nut, with melancholy sound.
Yet the low, moaning autumn wind, that sweeps
The seeded grass and lately-blossoming flower,
Bears the light germs of future life away,
And sows them by the gliding rivulet,
And o'er the plain, and on the mountain side,
To clothe anew the earth, when comes again
The quickening breath of spring. And on the place
Where fall the ripened nuts, the frosty night
Will heap the stricken leaves; and thence shall spring,
In many an after age, another growth
Of stately trees, when those around me now,
Fallen with eld, shall moulder, and enrich
The ground that now sustains their lofty pride.

Changing, forever changing!—So depart
The glories of the old majestic wood;
So pass the pride and garniture of fields;
The growth of ages, and the bloom of days,
Into the dust of centuries; and so
Are both renewed. The scattered tribes of men,
The generations of the populous earth,
All have their seasons too. And jocund Youth
Is the green spring-time—Manhood's lusty strength
Is the maturing summer—hoary Age
Types well the autumn of the year—and Death
Is the real winter, which forecloses all.
And shall the forests have another spring,
And shall the fields another garland wear,
And shall the worm come forth renew'd in life
And clothed with highest beauty, and not man?
No!—in the Book before me now, I read
Another language; and my faith is sure,
That though the chains of death may hold it long,
This mortal will o'ermaster them, and break
Away, and put on immortality.

Almighty Father! such the lesson is,
That, in these cool and venerable woods,
I con to-day; and firmer in my breast,
By every syllable, these truths are fixed:
That Thou art the beginning, and the end,
Of all this wondrous work; and that Thy love
Pervades the universe; and that Thy smile

Seeketh all hearts to sun them; and that Thou,
In every glorious thing we here behold,
Declarest and reveal'st Thyself to be
The Majesty Supreme—Eternal God.

ON A VALUED FRIEND.

BY JOHN M. HARNEY.

Devout, yet cheerful; pious, not austere;
To others lenient, to himself severe;
Tho' honored, modest; diffident, tho' prais'd;
The proud he humbled, and the humble rais'd;
Studious, yet social; though polite, yet plain;
No man more learned, yet no man less vain.
His fame would universal envy move,
But envy's lost in universal love.
That he has faults, it may be bold to doubt,
Yet certain 't is we ne'er have found them out.
If faults he has, (as man, 't is said, must have,)
They are the only faults he ne'er forgave.
I flatter not: absurd to flatter where
Just praise is fulsome, and offends the ear.

THE PROPHET'S DREAM.

BY JOHN B. DILLON.

"The land shall be utterly emptied, and utterly spoiled."—*Isaiah* xxiv, 3.

WHERE fell the palm-tree's clustering shade,
    The aged and weary Prophet lay,
And o'er his fevered temples played
    The freshness of the primal day.
He slept—and on his spirit fell
    A vision of the flight of Time—
He saw upon the future dwell
    A dark'ning cloud of sin and crime.

Gone were the spirits that lingered near
    The world in its early bloom,
And Hope's pure light, that was wont to cheer,
    Grew dim in the gathering gloom;
And Love from Earth was hurl'd—
      And a mandate came,
      In a breath of flame,
To scourge a sinful world.

"*Let the sword go forth!*"—and forth it went,
And gleamed o'er tower and battlement,
    And glanced in the tented field;
And helms were cleft, and shields were broke,
And breasts were bared to the battle stroke,
    Only in death to yield:

The warriors met—but not to part—
   And the sun glared redly on the scene;
And the broken sword, and the trampled heart,
   Might tell where the battle steed had been.
Dark and still, by the moon's pale beam,
   Lay mouldering heaps of slaughtered men—
The fountain of a sanguine stream—
   Earth drank the blood of her offspring then.

"*Go forth Disease!*"—and at the word,
The groans of a stricken world were heard,
   And the voice of woe rose high—
And myriads yielded up their breath,
As the haggard form of the tyrant Death
   On the rotten breeze swept by.
And the lovely green that overspread
   The world in its guiltless day,
Grew as deeply dark, and sear'd, and dead,
   As the parched earth, where it lay.
With lifeless limbs the livid trees
   Stood locked in the arms of Death,
Save one, that still to the withering breeze
   Could lend its poisonous breath.
Deeply the world, in that drear time,
Felt the deadly curse of sin and crime.

"*Famine go forth!*"—and at the name,
   Rose a feeble shriek, and a fearful laugh,
And a tottering, fleshless monster came,
   The lingering stream of life to quaff—

And he stalk'd o'er the earth, and the languid crowds
Were crush'd to the dust in their mildew'd shrouds:
Then rose the last of human groans,
As the shrivelled skin hung loose on the bones,
    And the stream of life was gone.
And Death expired on that awful day,
Where his slaughtered millions round him lay,
    For his fearful task was done.

Old Earth was lone—for her offspring lay
Mouldering dark on her bosom of clay—
    All tones of life were hushed—
And the brazen tombs of sepulchred men,
That battled the might of Time till then,
    Atom by atom were crushed—
And desolate round in its orbit whirl'd
The peopleless wreck of a worn-out world.

*   *   *   *   *   *   *

The dreamer woke, and the glorious day
    Broke calmly on his dream—
And the joyous birds from each green spray
    Caroll'd their morning hymn—
The Earth still moved in beauty there,
    With its clustering groves and emerald plains,
And the pure breeze bore the Prophet's prayer
    To the throne where the Rock of Ages reigns.

THE CLOSING YEAR.

BY GEORGE D. PRENTICE.

'Tis midnight's holy hour—and silence now
Is brooding like a gentle Spirit o'er
The still and pulseless world. Hark! on the winds
The bell's deep tones are swelling—'tis the knell
Of the departed year. No funeral train
Is sweeping past—yet, on the stream and wood,
With melancholy light, the moonbeams rest
Like a pale, spotless shroud—the air is stirred
As by a mourner's sigh—and on yon cloud,
That floats so still and placidly through heaven,
The Spirits of the Seasons seem to stand,
Young Spring, bright Summer, Autumn's solemn form,
And Winter with his aged locks, and breathe,
In mournful cadences that come abroad
Like the far wind-harp's wild and touching wail,
A melancholy dirge o'er the dead year
Gone from the Earth forever.

        "Tis a time
For memory and for tears. Within the deep
Still chambers of the heart, a spectre dim,
Whose tones are like the wizard voice of Time
Heard from the tomb of Ages, points its cold

And solemn finger to the beautiful
And holy visions, that have passed away
And left no shadow of their loveliness
On the dead waste of life. That spectre lifts
The coffin-lid of Hope, and Joy, and Love,
And, bending mournfully above the pale
Sweet forms, that slumber there, scatters dead flowers
O'er what has passed to nothingness. The year
Has gone, and, with it, many a glorious throng
Of happy dreams. Its mark is on each brow,
Its shadow in each heart. In its swift course,
It waved its sceptre o'er the beautiful—
And they are not. It laid its pallid hand
Upon the strong man—and the haughty form
Is fallen, and the flashing eye is dim.
It trod the hall of revelry, where thronged
The bright and joyous—and the tearful wail
Of stricken ones is heard where erst the song
And reckless shout resounded. It passed o'er
The battle-plain, where sword and spear and shield
Flashed in the light of mid-day—and the strength
Of serried hosts is shivered, and the grass,
Green from the soil of carnage, waves above
The crushed and mouldering skeleton. It came
And faded like a wreath of mist at eve;
Yet, ere it melted in the viewless air,
It heralded its millions to their home
In the dim land of dreams.

Remorseless Time—
Fierce Spirit of the Glass and Scythe—what power
Can stay him in his silent course, or melt
His iron heart to pity! On, still on,
He presses, and forever. The proud bird,
The condor of the Andes, that can soar
Through heaven's unfathomable depths, or brave
The fury of the northern hurricane,
And bathe his plumage in the thunder's home,
Furls his broad wings at nightfall, and sinks down
To rest upon his mountain crag—but Time
Knows not the weight of sleep or weariness,
And Night's deep darkness has no chain to bind
His rushing pinion. Revolutions sweep
O'er Earth, like troubled visions o'er the breast
Of dreaming sorrow—Cities rise and sink
Like bubbles on the water—Fiery isles
Spring blazing from the Ocean, and go back
To their mysterious caverns—Mountains rear
To heaven their bald and blackened cliffs, and bow
Their tall heads to the plain—New Empires rise,
Gathering the strength of hoary centuries,
And rush down like the Alpine avalanche,
Startling the nations—And the very stars,
Yon bright and burning blazonry of God,
Glitter a while in their eternal depths,
And, like the Pleiad, loveliest of their train,
Shoot from their glorious spheres and pass away
To darkle in the trackless void—Yet Time,

Time the Tomb-builder, holds his fierce career,
Dark, stern, all-pitiless, and pauses not
Amid the mighty wrecks that strew his path,
To sit and muse, like other conquerors,
Upon the fearful ruin he has wrought.

IMPROMPTU

ON RECEIVING A SPRIG OF HEART'S-EASE.

BY FREDERICK W. THOMAS.

How easy 'tis to give the flower,
    That emblems careless ease of heart;
Yet give the very gift the power
    To bid that careless ease depart.

For if forth from its budding leaves,
    Young, nestling Hope should breathe her sigh,
Too soon the trusting lover grieves
    To find the flower, and hope must die.

Then, Mary, ere again we part,
    Oh give me back the priceless dower—
The careless, happy ease of heart,
    That cheered me ere you gave the flower.

THE MOUNTAIN STORM.

BY NATHANIEL WRIGHT.

The friend of ease, in low-land grove,
May lull his cares, and tend his love;
See, but not mark, the languid plain,
A wide, a weary, blank domain;
In long and deep repose may view
Earth's pleasant green, and vault of blue,
Till soft he sinks, with sleep oppress'd,
Beneath th' untroubled sod to rest :—
Give me the scene of uproar wild!
The mountain cliffs in rudeness piled,
The summits bold, amid the sky,
Where the clouds pause, that journey by;
Or, as the storm's hoar torrent spreads,
Gambols the lightning round their heads;
The scene untamed, that fills the breast
With other feelings far than rest,
That tempts the thought to other charms,
Than Flora's lap, or Morpheus' arms,
And nerves the hand to other deed,
Than love's caress or Bacchus' meed.
Then ask not, why, with such delight,
I mark the scene round ———'s height.

Man—the poor insect of a day!
Just springs from earth to pass away,
Flits from the scene as light and fast,
As the lake's shadows in the blast:—
But mark yon hills! those cliffs have stood,
Unmoved, since round them dashed the flood.
How many a race, beneath their crest,
Has toiled its day, and gone to rest!

Skirting th' horizon's verge afar,
And neighbors of the evening star,
In varied form of peak or ridge,
Or woody dell, or naked ledge,
Here with a fleecy crest of cloud,
And there a dusky green-wood shroud;—
Approaching here, till field and cot
Distinctly mark the cultured spot,—
Retiring there, and soaring high,
And soft'ning, till they melt in sky,
The mountains spread:—too much like life,—
In passing, all turmoil and strife;
But seen at distance—pomp and pride,
Or joy and peace by parents' side.

Oft, when at eve the welcome rain
Has left its freshness on the plain,
A desert vast the dawn will greet,
Of sleeping cloud beneath your feet,
With here and there, a lonely head

Emerging from the ocean bed;
All else so lost, so still, and fair—
You almost ask if earth be there!
And wish the swallow's wing, to try
The magic flood, and bathe in sky.

But grander far the sable cloud,
Fraught with heaven's fire, and thunder loud;
Its fleecy van of silver sheen,
But all the rear a midnight scene;
The solemn peals, that slowly roll,
From north to south athwart the pole;
The bursting bolt, in vengeance hurl'd,
That jars this wide and solid world;
The pensile flash, whose vivid form
Crosses the blackness of the storm,
Descending now, with anger red,
Scathes the dark mountain's distant head,
Or plays its gambols round the sky,
A solemn scene to mortal eye!
The plains beneath with awe are still,
The wild bird screams not from the hill,
Grave is the lambkin in his cote,
And hushed the warbler's cheerful note.

At length th' advancing torrents mark
Yon utmost summits, veiled and dark,—
Hill after hill, as now it nears,
Is shaded—dimm'd—and disappears;

And mingle now along the plain,
The flash—the peal—and dashing rain.

The cloud has passed.—Descending day,
Beams forth its brightest, loveliest ray;—
The youthful flocks forget to feed,
Through joy's excess, and race the mead;
The songsters strain their little throats,
To lend their loudest, merriest notes;
And scarce that day does Phœbus part
From saddened eye, or sorrowing heart.

O! what were life's dull, transient hour,
Without its sunshine and its shower!
Its day of gloom, and doubt's dark dream,
And hope's succeeding, bright'ning beam?

Yet gaze once more!—The sun has set,
High tho' his rays are lingering yet—
How bright, beyond those summits old,
Spreads the broad field of living gold!
How black, upon that glowing vest,
Lie the long hills, that skirt the west!

Ambition, mark!—for glory's light
Even thus delays oblivion's night;—
A twilight splendor, soft and fair,
When death has veiled its fiercer glare;
But short the hour, and sure the lot,
It fades, it sinks, and is forgot.

WEDDED LOVE'S FIRST HOME.

BY JAMES HALL.

'Twas far beyond yon mountains, dear, we plighted vows of love;
The ocean wave was at our feet, the autumn sky above;
The pebbly shore was covered o'er, with many a varied shell,
And on the billow's curling spray, the sunbeams glittering fell.
The storm has vex'd that billow oft, and oft that sun has set,
But plighted love remains with us, in peace and lustre yet.

I wiled thee to a lonely haunt, that bashful love might speak
Where none could hear what love reveal'd, or see the crimson cheek;
The shore was all deserted, and we wandered there alone,
And not a human step impress'd the sand-beach but our own.
Thy footsteps all have vanished from the billow-beaten strand—
The vows we breathed remain with us—they were not traced in sand.

Far, far, we left the sea-girt shore, endeared by childhood's dream,
To seek the humble cot, that smiled by fair Ohio's stream;
In vain the mountain cliff opposed, the mountain torrent roar'd,

For love unfurl'd her silken wing, and o'er each barrier
　　soared;
And many a wide domain we pass'd and many an ample
　　dome,
But none so blessed, so dear to us, as wedded love's first
　　home.

Beyond those mountains now are all that e'er we loved or
　　knew,
The long remembered many, and the dearly cherish'd few;
The home of her we value, and the grave of him we mourn,
Are there;—and there is all the past to which the heart can
　　turn;—
But dearer scenes surround us here, and lovelier joys we
　　trace,
For here is wedded loves's first home,—its hallowed resting
　　place.

THE GOINGS FORTH OF GOD.

BY OTWAY CURRY.

GOD WALKETH ON THE EARTH. The purling rills
And mightier streams before him glance away,
Rejoicing in his presence. On the plains,
And spangled fields, and in the mazy vales,
The living throngs of earth before Him fall
With thankful hymns, receiving from his hand
Immortal life and gladness. Clothed upon
With burning crowns the mountain-heralds stand,
Proclaiming to the blossoming wilderness
The brightness of his coming, and the power
Of Him who ever liveth, all in all!

GOD WALKETH ON THE OCEAN. Brilliantly
The glassy waters mirror back His smiles.
The surging billows and the gamboling storms
Come crouching to His feet. The hoary deep,
And the green gorgeous islands, offer up
The tribute of their treasures—pearls, and shells,
And crown-like drapery of the flashing foam.
And solemnly the tesselated halls,
And coral domes of mansions in the depths,
And gardens of the golden sanded seas,
Blend, with the anthems of the chiming waves,

Their alleluias unto Him who rules
The invisible armies of eternity.

GOD JOURNEYETH IN THE SKY. From sun to sun,
From star to star the living lightnings flash;
And pealing thunders through all space proclaim
The goings forth of Him whose potent arm
Perpetuates existence, or destroys.
From depths unknown, unsearchable, profound,
Forth rush the wandering comets: girt with flames
They blend, in order true, with marshalling hosts
Of starry worshippers. The unhallowed orbs
Of earth-born fire that cleave the hazy air,
Blanched by the flood of uncreated light,
Fly with the fleeting winds and misty clouds
Back to their homes, and deep in darkness lie.

GOD JOURNEYETH IN THE HEAVENS. Refulgent stars,
And glittering crowns of prostrate Seraphim,
Emboss his burning path. Around Him fall
Dread powers, dominions, hosts, and kingly thrones.
Angels of God—adoring millions—join
With spirits pure, redeem'd from distant worlds,
In choral songs of praise.—"Thee we adore,
For Thou art mighty. Everlasting spheres
Of light and glory in thy presence wait.
Time, space, life, light, dominion, majesty,
Truth, wisdom—all are thine, Jehovah! Thou
FIRST, LAST, SUPREME, ETERNAL POTENTATE!"

TO A POETESS.

BY THOMAS H. SHREVE.

Hail, gifted one of song!
Whose harp, breathed on by the inspiring Nine,
Pours its rich stream of melody divine,
    Our western land along!

    Genius, proud girl, is thine!
Thou wav'st thy sceptre o'er far fairy land,
And to thy brow full many a flowery band
    Come up as to a shrine!

    Girl of the eagle eye!
No earth-born mists thy searching vision shroud,
But far beyond the tempest and the cloud
    Thy raptured glances fly.

    The clime of song to thee,
Wears not the sable hue of starless night,
But in its beauty bursts upon thy sight,
    From blinding shadows free.

    Before thy dreaming mind
Ideal forms in all their glory play,
More beautiful than clouds that melt away
    Upon the summer's wind.

Upon thy eager ear
Falls melody as soft as Siren's tones,
When through the shadowy woods the wild wind moans
    O'er the departing year.

Then oft at dewy eve
Thy spirit soareth up on seraph wing,
And drinking bliss at thought's perennial spring,
    Forgets that earth can grieve.

Thy brow is eloquent
Of those high thoughts that, star-like, ever gleam
Above the voyagers on life's dark stream,
    Like blessings heaven-sent.

Thy spirit finds in flowers,
In songs of birds, in stars that gem the night,
And autumn winds that earth's green glories blight,
    Friends for its lonely hours.

Oh, may thy Life's tide flow
As smoothly on as some glad song of thine,
Begemm'd by flowers, and mirroring things divine,
    Without a shade of woe.

TASSO — IN PRISON.

BY JAMES H. PERKINS.

Yes, I am chained: these dark and dreary walls
   Must henceforth my horizon be; no light
Will ever come to cheer my aching balls,
Save 'tis the jailor's torch, flashing along
   The firm-ribbed archway, as he comes at night
To deal me out my pittance. I was strong,—
Strong once, in mind and frame: 'tis gone, and now
I have no power; 'tis gone, I know not how:
It cannot be that servitude hath might
To rob the spirit of its heaven-born flight,
   And plunge the mind in an eternal night?
Let me not think of such things, for my brain
   Is weak, and when I think, upon my sight
Those chilling visions all crowd back again,
As to the murderer's eye the spirits of the slain.

Yes, I am chained: the mountain stream no more
   Will bear me on its bosom; ne'er again
Shall I go down at evening to the shore,
To listen to the chaféd ocean's roar;
   Nor ever climb the mottled hill-side, when
The thunder clouds are gathering; nor repose
   By the calm lake at evening, when the earth

Is hushed, to hear that music from above,
Which wins the sorrowing from his want and woes,
   In the desponding breeds a holy mirth,
And in the hating breast calls forth a fount of love.

Yes, I am chained; but are not all men so?
   Are they not chains, these passions frail yet foul?
Is not the body we are wedded to,
   A clog upon the still upspringing soul?
Then am I freer than my tyrant lord,
For I have crush'd this body, I have poured
My spirit into that which I adored,—
   My mother Nature;—fettered, I have broke
Free from the earthly bonds, and foul desires,
   Which cling around us, as the parasite
Clings to and crushes in its poisonous spires
   The strength and beauty of the heavenward oak.
I am a freeman! I can take my flight
   With the Great Spirit, to the realms above,
And ride upon the whirlwind; I am part
   And portion of Thee, Author of all love;
I shall be present whereso'er Thou art;
   In the far west, at sunset; on the wave
When the storm waketh; in the bursting bud,
The flower, the withering leaf, the angry flood;
The birth, the bridal, and the field of blood;
   In life and death,—the cradle and the grave.

TECUMSEH.

BY CHARLES A. JONES.

Where rolls the dark and turbid Thames
   His consecrated wave along,
Sleeps one, than whose, few are the names
   More worthy of the lyre and song;
Yet o'er whose spot of lone repose
   No pilgrim eyes are seen to weep;
And no memorial marble throws
   Its shadow where his ashes sleep.

Stop, stranger! there Tecumseh lies;
   Behold the lowly resting place
Of all that of the hero dies;
   The Cæsar—Tully—of his race:
Whose arm of strength, and fiery tongue,
   Have won him an immortal name,
And from the mouths of millions wrung
   Reluctant tribute to his fame.

Stop—for 'tis glory claims thy tear!
   True worth belongs to all mankind:
And he whose ashes slumber here,
   Though man in form was god in mind.

What matter he was not like thee,
    In race and color—'tis the soul
That marks man's true divinity—
    Then let not shame thy tears control.

Art thou a patriot?—so was he!
    His breast was Freedom's holiest shrine;
And as thou bendest there thy knee,
    His spirit will unite with thine.
All that a man can give, he gave—
    His life—the country of his sires
From the oppressor's grasp to save:
    In vain—quench'd are his nation's fires.

Art thou a soldier? dost thou not
    O'er deeds chivalric love to muse?
Here stay thy steps—what better spot
    Couldst thou for contemplation choose?
The earth beneath is holy ground;
    It holds a thousand valiant braves;
Tread lightly o'er each little mound,
    For they are no ignoble graves.

Thermopylæ and Marathon,
    Though classic earth, can boast no more
Of deeds heroic than yon sun
    Once saw upon this lonely shore,
When in a gallant nation's last
    And deadliest struggle, for its own,

  Tecumseh's fiery spirit pass'd
   In blood, and sought its Father's throne.

Oh, softly fall the summer dew,
 The tears of heaven, upon his sod,
For he in life and death was true,
 Both to his country and his God;
For oh, if God to man has given,
 From his bright home beyond the skies,
One feeling that's akin to heaven,
 'Tis his who for his country dies.

Rest, warrior, rest!—Though not a dirge
 Is thine, beside the wailing blast,
Time cannot in oblivion merge
 The light thy star of glory cast;
While heave yon high hills to the sky,
 While rolls yon dark and turbid river,
Thy name and fame can never die—
 Whom Freedom loves will live forever.

EXTRACT FROM 'THE EMIGRANT.'

BY FREDERICK W. THOMAS.

Here once Boone trod—the hardy Pioneer—
The only whiteman in the wilderness :
Oh ! how he loved, alone, to hunt the deer,
Alone at eve, his simple meal to dress ;
No mark upon the tree, nor print, nor track,
To lead him forward, or to guide him back :
He roved the forest, king by main and might,
And looked up to the sky and shaped his course aright.

That mountain, there, that lifts its bald high head
Above the forest, was, perchance, his throne ;
There has he stood and marked the woods outspread,
Like a great kingdom, that was all his own ;
In hunting shirt and moccasins arrayed,
With bear-skin cap, and pouch, and needful blade.
How carelessly he lean'd upon his gun !
That sceptre of the wild, that had so often won.

Those western Pioneers an impulse felt,
Which their less hardy sons scarce comprehend ;
Alone, in Nature's wildest scenes they dwelt ;
Where crag, and precipice, and torrent blend,
And stretched around the wilderness, as rude
As the red rovers of its solitude,

Who watched their coming with a hate profound,
And fought with deadly strife for every inch of ground.

To shun a greater ill sought they the wild?
No, they left happier lands behind them far,
And brought the nursing mother and her child
To share the dangers of the border war;
The log-built cabin from the Indian barred,
Their little boy, perchance, kept watch and ward,
While father ploughed with rifle at his back,
Or sought the glutted foe through many a devious track.

How cautiously, yet fearlessly, that boy
Would search the forest for the wild beast's lair,
And lift his rifle with a hurried joy,
If chance he spied the Indian lurking there:
And should they bear him prisoner from the fight,
While they are sleeping, in the dead midnight,
He slips the thongs that bind him to the tree,
And leaving death with them, bounds home right happily.

Before the mother, bursting through the door,
The red man rushes where her infants rest;
O God! he hurls them on the cabin floor!
While she, down kneeling, clasps them to her breast.
How he exults and revels in her woe,
And lifts the weapon, yet delays the blow;
Ha! that report! behold! he reels! he dies!
And quickly to her arms the husband—father—flies.

LOVE'S CONSTANCY.

BY CHARLES D. DRAKE.

The flower that oft beneath the ray
    Of sunlit warmth has bloomed,
Will fade and shrink from life away
    If to a dungeon doomed:—
But even here, should chance disclose
    Some beam of genial light,
Its head to that the dying rose
    Will turn from gloom and night.

The cord that, gently touched, will thrill
    With music's softest strain,
If rudely swept, at careless will,
    Gives forth no note again;
But still there lingers on the ear
    A low, faint, murmuring swell,
As if the tone would yet be near
    Where once 'twas wont to dwell.

So from the heart that once has known
    Love's impulse and its power,
Though light may be forever flown,
    As from the imprisoned flower;

Forever still its gaze will be
    Where first was seen its star,
As shipwrecked men on shoreless sea
    Yearn to their homes afar:
Still like the bud that, crushed, will yield
    Its sweetest fragrance last,
The heart that once to love has kneeled,
    Will love though hope be past!

SONNET.

BY GEORGE B. WALLIS.

Wilson, a chapter in thy luring book
    Of ornithology, and I shall be
Driving the sedge-hen down the rumbling brook,
    Or winding flankward on a shy kildee;
For, while unwillingly I move within
The focus of a city's smoke and din,
    The page is welcome as the forest dell.
And I could wish to sit upon thy tomb,
When Evening's cheek was purpling into bloom,
    To hear the gathering birds in concert swell
Their dirge above thee. From thy cage of gloom,
    May thy freed spirit, newly fledged, arise,
On Time's departing morn, a Bird of Paradise.

TO THE MOCKING BIRD.

BY ALBERT PIKE.

Thou glorious mocker of the world! I hear
Thy many voices ringing through the glooms
Of these green solitudes—and all the clear,
Bright joyance of their song enthralls the ear
And floods the heart. Over the sphered tombs
Of vanished nations rolls thy music tide.
No light from history's starlike page illumes
The memory of those nations—they have died.
None cares for them but thou—and thou mayst sing,
Perhaps, o'er me—as now thy song doth ring
Over their bones by whom thou once wast deified.

Thou scorner of all cities! Thou dost leave
The world's turmoil and never-ceasing din,
Where one from other's no existence weaves,
Where the old sighs, the young turns grey and grieves,
Where misery gnaws the maiden's heart within:
And thou dost flee into the broad green woods,
And with thy soul of music thou dost win
Their heart to harmony—no jar intrudes
Upon thy sounding melody. Oh, where,
Amid the sweet musicians of the air,
Is one so dear as thee to these old solitudes?

Ha! what a burst was that! the Æolian strain
Goes floating through the tangled passages
Of the lone woods—and now it comes again—
A multitudinous melody—like a rain
Of glossy music under echoing trees,
Over a ringing lake; it wraps the soul
With a bright harmony of happiness—
Even as a gem is wrapt, when round it roll
Their waves of brilliant flame—till we become,
Ev'n with the excess of our deep pleasure, dumb,
And pant like some swift runner clinging to the goal.

I cannot love the man who doth not love,
(Even as men love light,) the song of birds:
For the first visions that my boy-heart wove,
To fill its sleep with, were, that I did rove
Amid the woods—what time the snowy herds
Of morning cloud fled from the rising sun
Into the depths of heaven's heart; as words
That from the poet's tongue do fall upon
And vanish in the human heart; and then
I revelled in those songs, and sorrowed, when
With noon-heat overwrought, the music's burst was done.

I would, sweet bird! that I might live with thee,
Amid the eloquent grandeur of the shades,
Alone with nature—but it may not be;
I have to struggle with the tumbling sea
Of human life, until existence fades

Into death's darkness. Thou wilt sing and soar
Thro' the thick woods and shadow-chequered glades,
While nought of sorrow casts a dimness o'er
The brilliance of thy heart—but I must wear,
As now, my garmenting of pain and care—
As penitents of old their galling sackcloth wore.

Yet why complain?—What though fond hopes deferr'd
Have overshadowed Youth's green paths with gloom!
Still, joy's rich music is not all unheard,—
There is a voice sweeter than thine, sweet bird!
To welcome me, within my humble home;—
There is an eye with love's devotion bright,
The darkness of existence to illume!
Then why complain?—When death shall cast his blight
Over the spirit, then my bones shall rest
Beneath these trees—and from thy swelling breast,
O'er them thy song shall pour like a rich flood of light.

LINES ON PASSING THE GRAVE OF MY SISTER.

BY MICAH P. FLINT.

On yonder shore, on yonder shore,
    Now verdant with the depths of shade,
Beneath the white-armed sycamore,
    There is a little infant laid.
Forgive this tear.—A brother weeps.—
'Tis there the faded floweret sleeps.

She sleeps alone, she sleeps alone,
    And summer's forests o'er her wave;
And sighing winds at autumn moan
    Around the little stranger's grave,
As though they murmured at the fate
Of one so lone and desolate.

In sounds that seem like sorrow's own,
    Their funeral dirges faintly creep;
Then deep'ning to an organ tone,
    In all their solemn cadence sweep,
And pour, unheard, along the wild,
Their desert anthem o'er a child.

She came, and passed. Can I forget,
  How we whose hearts had hailed her birth,
Ere three autumnal suns had set,
  Consigned her to her mother Earth!
Joys and their memories pass away;
But griefs are deeper ploughed than they.

We laid her in her narrow cell,
  We heaped the soft mould on her breast;
And parting tears, like rain-drops, fell
  Upon her lonely place of rest.
May angels guard it:—may they bless
Her slumbers in the wilderness.

She sleeps alone, she sleeps alone:
  For, all unheard, on yonder shore,
The sweeping flood, with torrent moan,
  At evening lifts its solemn roar,
As, in one broad, eternal tide,
The rolling waters onward glide.

There is no marble monument,
  There is no stone, with graven lie,
To tell of love and virtue blent
  In one almost too good to die.
We needed no such useless trace
To point us to her resting place.

She sleeps alone, she sleeps alone ;
   But, midst the tears of April showers,
The genius of the wild hath strown
   His germs of fruits, his fairest flowers,
And cast his robes of vernal bloom
In guardian fondness o'er her tomb.

She sleeps alone, she sleeps alone ;
   Yet yearly is her grave-turf dress'd,
And still the summer vines are thrown,
   In annual wreaths, across her breast,
And still the sighing autumn grieves,
And strews the hallowed spot with leaves.

THE MOTHERS OF THE WEST.

BY WILLIAM D. GALLAGHER.

The Mothers of our Forest-Land!
  Stout-hearted dames were they;
With nerve to wield the battle-brand,
  And join the border-fray.
Our rough land had no braver,
  In its days of blood and strife—
Aye ready for severest toil,
  Aye free to peril life.

The Mothers of our Forest-Land!
  On old Kan-tuc-kee's soil,
How shared they, with each dauntless band,
  War's tempest and Life's toil!
They shrank not from the foeman—
  They quailed not in the fight—
But cheer'd their husbands through the day,
  And soothed them through the night.

The Mothers of our Forest-Land!
  Their bosoms pillowed *men!*
And proud were they by such to stand,
  In hammock, fort, or glen.

To load the sure old rifle—
    To run the leaden ball—
To watch a battling husband's place,
    And fill it should he fall:

The Mothers of our Forest-Land!
    Such were their daily deeds.
Their monument!—where does it stand?
    Their epitaph!—who reads?
No braver dames had Sparta,
    No nobler matrons Rome—
Yet who or lauds or honors them,
    Ev'n in their own green home!

The Mothers of our Forest-Land!
    They sleep in unknown graves:
And had they borne and nursed a band
    Of ingrates, or of slaves,
They had not been more neglected!
    But their graves shall yet be found,
And their monuments dot here and there
    "The Dark and Bloody Ground."

ON SEEING AN INFANT SLEEPING ON ITS MOTHER'S BOSOM.

BY MRS. AMELIA B. WELBY.

It lay upon its mother's breast, a thing
   Bright as a dew-drop when it first descends,
Or as the plumage of an angel's wing
   Where every tint of rainbow-beauty blends;
It had soft violet eyes, that, 'neath each lid
   Half closed upon them, like bright waters shone,
While its small dimpled hands were slyly hid
   In the warm bosom that it nestled on.

There was a beam in that young mother's eye,
   Lit by the feelings that she could not speak,
As from her lips a plaintive lullaby
   Stirred the bright tresses on her infant's cheek,
While now and then with melting heart she prest
   Soft kisses o'er its red and smiling lips—
Lips, sweet as rose-buds in fresh beauty dress'd
   Ere the young murmuring bee their honey sips.

It was a fragrant eve; the sky was full
   Of burning stars, that tremulously clear
Shone on those lovely ones, while the low lull
   Of falling waters fell upon the ear;

And the new moon, like a pure shell of pearl
　　Encircled by the blue waves of the deep,
Lay mid the fleecy clouds that love to curl
　　Around the stars when they their vigils keep.

My heart grew softer as I gazed upon
　　That youthful mother, as she soothed to rest
With a low song her loved and cherished one—
　　The bud of promise on her gentle breast;
For 't is a sight that angel ones above
　　May stoop to gaze on from their bowers of bliss,
When Innocence upon the breast of Love
　　Is cradled, in a sinful world like this.

THE WIFE.

BY MRS. ANNE P. DINNIES.

"She flung her white arms round him—Thou art all that this poor heart can cling to."

I could have stemm'd misfortune's tide,
   And borne the rich one's sneer,
Have braved the haughty glance of pride,
   Nor shed a single tear:
I could have smiled on every blow
   From Life's full quiver thrown,
While I might gaze on thee, and know
   I should not be 'alone.'

I could—I think I could have brook'd,
   E'en for a time, that thou
Upon my fading face had'st look'd
   With less of love than now;
For then I should at least have felt
   The sweet hope still my own,
To win thee back, and, whilst I dwelt
   On earth, not be 'alone.'

But thus to see, from day to day,
   Thy brightening eye and cheek,
And watch thy life-sands waste away,
   Unnumbered, slowly, meek;

To meet thy smiles of tenderness,
  And catch the feeble tone
Of kindness, ever breathed to bless,
  And feel, I'll be ' alone ;'—

To mark thy strength each hour decay,
  And yet thy hopes grow stronger,
As, filled with heaven-ward trust, they say,
  " Earth may not claim thee longer ;"
Nay, dearest, 't is too much—this heart
  Must break, when thou art gone ;
It must not be ; we may not part ;
  I could not live ' alone !'

ON CROSSING THE ALLEGHANIES.

BY MRS. LAURA M. THURSTON.

The broad, the bright, the glorious West,
  Is spread before me now!
Where the gray mists of morning rest
  Beneath yon mountain's brow!
The bound is past—the goal is won—
The region of the setting sun
  Is open to my view.
Land of the valiant and the free—
My own Green Mountain land—to thee,
  And thine, a long adieu!

I hail thee, Valley of the West,
  For what thou yet shalt be!
I hail thee for the hopes that rest
  Upon thy destiny!
Here—from this mountain height, I see
Thy bright waves floating to the sea,
  Thine emerald fields outspread,
And feel that in the book of fame,
Proudly shall thy recorded name
  In later days be read.

Yet while I gaze upon thee now,
  All glorious as thou art,

A cloud is resting on my brow,
   A weight upon my heart.
To me—in all thy youthful pride—
Thou art a land of cares untried,
   Of untold hopes and fears.
Thou art—yet not for thee I grieve;
But for the far-off land I leave,
   I look on thee with tears.

O! brightly, brightly, glow thy skies,
   In summer's sunny hours!
The green earth seems a paradise
   Arrayed in summer flowers!
But oh! there is a land afar
Whose skies to me are brighter far
   Along the Atlantic shore!
For eyes beneath their radiant shrine,
In kindlier glances answered mine—
   Can these their light restore?

Upon the lofty bound I stand,
   That parts the East and West;
Before me—lies a fairy land;
   Behind—*a home of rest!*
Here, hope her wild enchantment flings,
Portrays all bright and lovely things,
   My footsteps to allure—
But *there,* in memory's light, I see
All that was once most dear to me—
   My young heart's cynosure!

THE FEVER DREAM.

BY JOHN M. HARNEY.

A FEVER scorched my body, fired my brain!
Like lava in Vesuvius, boiled my blood
Within the glowing caverns of my heart.
I raged with thirst, and begged a cold, clear draught
Of fountain water.—'T was with tears denied.
I drank a nauseous febrifuge, and slept;
But rested not—harassed with horrid dreams
Of burning deserts, and of dusty plains,
Mountains disgorging flames—forests on fire,
Steam, sun-shine, smoke, and boiling lakes—
Hills of hot sand, and glowing stones that seemed
Embers and ashes of a burnt up world!

Thirst raged within me.—I sought the deepest vale,
And called on all the rocks and caves for water;—
I climbed a mountain, and from cliff to cliff
Pursued a flying cloud, howling for water:—
I crushed the withered herbs, and gnawed dry roots,
Still crying, Water! water!—While the cliffs and caves,
In horrid mockery, re-echoed " Water!"
Below the mountain gleamed a city, red
With solar flame, upon the sandy bank
Of a broad river.—" Soon, oh soon!" I cried,

"I'll cool my burning body in that flood,
And quaff my fill."—I ran—I reached the shore.
The river was dried up. Its oozy bed
Was dust; and on its arid rocks, I saw
The scaly myriads fry beneath the sun!
Where sank the channel deepest, I beheld
A stirring multitude of human forms,
And heard a faint, wild, lamentable wail.
Thither I sped, and joined the general cry
Of—" water!" They had delved a spacious pit
In search of hidden fountains—sad, sad sight!
I saw them rend the rocks up in their rage,
With mad impatience calling on the earth
To open and yield up her cooling fountains.

Meanwhile the skies, on which they dared not gaze,
Stood o'er them like a canopy of brass—
Undimmed by moisture. The red dog-star raged,
And Phœbus from the house of Virgo shot
His scorching shafts. The thirsty multitude
Grew still more frantic. Those who dug the earth
Fell lifeless on the rocks they strained to upheave,
And filled again, with their own carcasses,
The pits they made—undoing their own work!
Despair at length drove out the laborers,
At sight of whom a general groan announced
The death of hope. Ah! now no more was heard
The cry of "water!" To the city next,
Howling, we ran—all hurrying without aim :—

Thence to the woods. The baked plain gaped for moisture,
And from its arid breast heaved smoke, that seemed
The breath of furnace—fierce, volcanic fire,
Or hot monsoon, that raises Syrian sands
To clouds. Amid the forests we espied
A faint and bleating herd. Sudden a shrill
And horrid shout arose of "Blood! blood! blood!"
We fell upon them with a tiger's thirst,
And drank up all the blood that was not human!
We were dyed in blood! Despair returned;
The cry of blood was hushed, and dumb confusion reigned.
Even then, when hope was dead!—past hope—
I heard a laugh! and saw a wretched man
Rip his own veins, and bleeding, drink
With eager joy. The example seized on all:—
Each fell upon himself, tearing his veins
Fiercely in search of blood! And some there were,
Who, having emptied their own veins, did seize
Upon their neighbors' arms, and slew them for their blood.
Oh! happy then were mothers who gave suck.
They dashed their little infants from their breasts,
And their shrunk bosoms tortured to extract
The balmy juice, oh! exquisitely sweet
To their parched tongues! 'T is done!—now all is gone!
Blood, water, and the bosom's nectar,—all!

"Rend, oh! ye lightnings! the sealed firmament,
And flood a burning world.—Rain! rain! pour! pour!
Open—ye windows of high heaven! and pour

The mighty deluge! Let us drown, and drink
Luxurious death! Ye earthquakes split the globe,
The solid, rock-ribbed globe!—and lay all bare
Its subterranean rivers, and fresh seas!"

Thus raged the multitude. And many fell
In fierce convulsions ;—many slew themselves.

And now I saw the city all in flames—
The forest burning—and the very earth on fire!
I saw the mountains open with a roar,
Loud as the seven apocalyptic thunders,
And seas of lava rolling headlong down,
Through crackling forests fierce, and hot as hell,
Down to the plain.—I turned to fly,——and waked!

OUR EARLY DAYS.

BY WILLIAM D. GALLAGHER.

OUR EARLY DAYS!—How often back
We turn on Life's bewildering track,
To where, o'er hill and valley, plays
The sunlight of our early days!

A Boy!—my truant steps were seen
Where streams were bright, and meadows green;
Where flow'rs, in beauty and perfume,
Breath'd ever of the Eden-bloom,—
And birds, abroad in the free wind,
Sang, as they left the earth behind
And wing'd their joyous way above,
Of Eden-peace, and Eden-love.
That life was of the soul, as well
As of the outward-visible;
And now, its streams are dry; and sere,
And brown, its meadows all appear;
Gone are its flow'rs; its bird's glad voice
But seldom bids my heart rejoice;
And, like the mist as comes the day,
Its Eden-glories roll away.

A Youth!—the mountain torrent made
The music which my soul obey'd.
To shun the crowded ways of men,
And seek the old tradition'd glen,
Where, through the dim, uncertain light,
Moved many an ever-changing sprite,—
Alone the splinter'd crag to dare,
While trooping shadows fill'd the air,
And quicken'd fancy many a form
Traced vaguely in the gathering storm,—
To tread the forest's lone arcades,
And dream of Sherwood's peopled shades,
And Windsor's haunted 'alleys green'
'Dingle' and 'bosky bourn' between,
Till burst upon my raptured glance
The whole wide realm of Old Romance:
Such was the life I lived—a youth!
But vanish'd, at the touch of Truth,
And never to be known agen,
Is all that made my being then.

A Man!—the thirst for fame was mine,
And bow'd me at Ambition's shrine,
Among the votaries who have given
Time, health, hope, peace—and madly striven,
Ay, madly! for that which, when found,
Is oftenest but an empty sound.

And I have worshipp'd!—even yet
Mine eye is on the Idol set;
But it hath found so much to be
But hollowness and mockery,
That from its worship oft it turns
To where a Light intenser burns,
Before whose radiance, pure and warm,
Ambition's star must cease to charm.

Our early days!—They haunt us ever—
Bright star-gleams on Life's silent river,
Which pierce the shadows, deep and dun,
That bar e'en manhood's noonday sun.

THE MINSTREL'S HOME.

BY OTWAY CURRY.

The image of a happier home,
    Whence far my feet have stray'd,
Still flits around me, as I roam,
    Like Joy's departed shade;—
Though childhood's light of joy has set,
Its home is dear to memory yet!

Here—where the lapse of time hath swept
    The forest's waving pride,
And many a summer's light hath slept
    Upon the green hill's side,
I'll rest—while twilight's pinions spread
Their shadows o'er my grassy bed.

Yon stars—enthroned so high—so bright,
    Like gems on heaven's fair brow,
Through all the majesty of night
    Are smiling on me now:
The promptings of poetic dreams
Are floating on their pale, pure beams.

The Muses of the starry spheres
    High o'er me wend along,
With visions of my infant years
    Blending their choral song—

Strewing with fancy's choicest flowers,
The pathway of the trancéd hours.

They sing of constellations high,
    The weary minstrel's home ;
Of days of sorrow hastening by,
    And bright ones yet to come—
Far in the sky, like ocean isles,
Where sunny light forever smiles.

They sing of happy circles, bright,
    Where bards of old have gone ;
Where rounding ages of delight,
    Undimm'd, are shining on ;—
And now, in silence, sleeps again
The breathing of their mystic strain.

Leave me—O ! leave me not alone,
    While I am sleeping here ;
Still let that soft and silvery tone
    Sound in my dreaming ear:
I would not lose that strain divine,
To call earth's thousand kingdoms mine !

It is the sunbeam of the mind,
    Whose bliss can ne'er be won,
Till the reviving soul shall find
    Life's long, dark journey done,—
Then peerless splendor shall array
The morning of that sinless day.

MIDNIGHT MUSINGS.

BY THOMAS H. SHREVE.

Lone midnight comes apace. The wakeful winds,
Like whispering spirits, momently flit by
With tones so soft that Peace unstartled sits
On the deep bosom of the solemn Night.
The burning stars are looking from their heights,
And seem so clear to sense, to thought so pure,
That mind needs not the talismanic wand
Of poetry divine to crowd their courts
With hosts of seraphim, and harps of love.

Deep as the distant thunder's awful tone,
And solemn as a funeral note, the dirge
Of a departing year swells on the wind.
Among its blending scenes of light and shade,
Some things there were which may not be forgot,
But which, graved on the inmost sense, shall live
Until the busy heart has ceased to heave
A sigh o'er pleasures lost, and the torn soul,
Escaping from its ligaments of clay,
Shall, on immortal pinions, rise aloft
And soar beyond the faintly glimmering stars
That gem the blue immensity of space.
'T is true that Time with slow remission steals
The pang from common grief, yet there is woe
Beyond the great Magician's skill to heal,

Which stamps itself deep in the central heart,
And, like the fissure in the ocean rock,
Resists the waves of the Lethean sea.

There is a beauty on Night's queen-like brow,
With her rich jewelry of blazing stars,
That to the heart which yearns for purer scenes
And holier love than greets it here, appeals
With a resistless force. Great Nature then
Asserts her empire o'er the souls of those,
Her favored children, on whose eager ears
There falls no wind which hath not melody,
And to whose eyes each star unfolds a world
Of glory and of bliss. The poet feels
The inspiration of an hour like this,
When silence like a garment wraps the earth,
And when the soundless air seems populous
With gentle spirits hovering o'er the haunts
Which most they loved while prisoned in their clay.
The mysteries of the universe then woo
His mind, and lead it up from height to height
Of lofty speculation, to the Throne
Round which all suns and worlds and systems roll.
The Past for him unlocks her affluent stores,
And human crowds long gathered home by death
To his dark kingdom, people earth again.
Palmyra rears her towers above the dust
And proudly points her glittering spires to heaven—
Rome Rises up and seems as once she was,
Her haughty eagles floating o'er her hills

And flashing back the gaudy light of day
Into the blue above—and Babylon
Lifts up her head, and o'er her gardens wide
The south wind wantons, while her massive gates
Swing on their hinges as the human tide
Beats up against them. Thus rapt fancy oft
Doth build again what, with his iron heel,
Wild Ruin ground into the very dust,
Which cloud-like rises on the tempest's wings
As it all-conquering sweeps the desert's waste.
Such is the talismanic power divine
Of Genius over death and time and space.
It reads the dim memorials on the tombs
Of buried empires—peoples solitudes—
And sways its sceptre o'er the realms of night.
In its blest missions to the homes of men
It turns aside from palaces and pomp,
And gently stoops to kiss the pearly brow
Of the boy peasant 'neath the humblest roof.
With eye anointed, it hath read the stars,
And traced out on the boundless blue of heaven
The wanderings of worlds. Its voice goes forth,
And o'er the billows of time's wasteful sea
It rolleth on forever. It hath sung
Old Ocean's praise, and with his surges' roar
Its song will ever mingle. It hath poured
A flood of radiance over hill and stream,
And reared a fiery pillar in the sky,
To light the nations on their pilgrimage
From darkness into everlasting day.

SPRING VERSES.

BY WILLIAM D. GALLAGHER.

How with the song of every bird,
    And with the scent of every flow'r,
Some recollection dear is stirr'd
    Of many a long-departed hour,
Whose course, though shrouded now in night,
Was traced in lines of golden light!

I know not if, when years have cast
    Their shadows on life's early dreams,
'T is wise to touch the Hope that 's past,
    And re-illume its fading beams:
But, though the future hath its star,
That olden Hope is dearer far.

Of all the present, much is bright;
    And in the coming years, I see
A brilliant and a cheering light,
    Which burns before me constantly,—
Guiding my steps, through haze and gloom,
To where Fame's turrets proudly loom.

Yet coldly shines it on my brow;
    And in my breast it wakes to life

None of the holy feelings now,
　　With which my boyhood's heart was rife:
It cannot touch that secret spring
Which erst made life so bless'd a thing.

Give me—then give me birds and flow'rs,
　　Which are the voice and breath of Spring!
For those the songs of life's young hours
　　With thrilling touch recall and sing,—
And these, with their sweet breath, impart
Old tales, whose memory warms the heart.

―――――

SPIRITUAL PRESENCE.

BY JAMES H. PERKINS.

It is a beautiful belief,
That ever round our head
Are hovering, on noiseless wing,
The spirits of the dead.

It is a beautiful belief,
When ended our career,
That it will be our ministry
To watch o'er others here;

To lend a moral to the flower;
Breathe wisdom on the wind;
To hold commune, at night's pure noon,
With the imprison'd mind;

To bid the mourners cease to mourn,
The trembling be forgiven;
To bear away, from ills of clay,
The infant to its heaven.

Ah! when delight was found in life,
And joy in every breath,
I cannot tell how terrible
The mystery of death.

But now the past is bright to me,
And all the future clear;
For 't is my faith, that after death
I still shall linger here.

THE OLD MOUND.*

BY CHARLES A. JONES.

Lonely and sad it stands:
The trace of ruthless hands
Is on its sides and summit, and around
The dwellings of the white man pile the ground;
And curling in the air,
The smoke of thrice a thousand hearths is there:
Without, all speaks of life,—within,
Deaf to the city's echoing din,
Sleep well the tenants of that silent mound,
Their names forgot, their memories unrenown'd.

Upon its top I tread,
And see around me spread
Temples and mansions, and the hoary hills,
Bleak with the labor that the coffer fills,
But mars their bloom the while,
And steals from nature's face its joyous smile:
And here and there, below,
The stream's meandering flow
Breaks on the view; and westward in the sky
The gorgeous clouds in crimson masses lie.

---

* In the western part of Cincinnati—nearly demolished years ago by a vandal curiosity, and now utterly neglected.

The hammer's clang rings out,
　　　Where late the Indian's shout
Startled the wild-fowl from its sedgy nest,
And broke the wild deer's and the panther's rest.
　　　The lordly oaks went down
Before the axe—the canebrake is a town:
　　　The bark canoe no more
　　　Glides noiseless from the shore;
And, sole memorial of a nation's doom,
Amid the works of art rises this lonely tomb.

　　　It too must pass away:
　　　Barbaric hands will lay
Its holy ruins level with the plain,
And rear upon its site some goodly fane.
　　　It seemeth to upbraid
The white man for the ruin he has made.
　　　And soon the spade and mattock must
　　　Invade the sleepers' buried dust,
And bare their bones to sacrilegious eyes,
And send them forth some joke-collector's prize.

THE REVOLUTIONERS.

BY GEORGE B. WALLIS.

As stars before the morning's light
    With the thin azure seem to mix;
Thus ye are fading from our sight,
    Spirits of Seventy-Six.

And, veterans of that stormy strife,
    A health to you: "A nation's praise
Gladden the winter of your life,
    The evening of your days."

Fathers of Freedom! ye have built
    A temple worthy of your stock;
Cemented by the blood ye spilt
    Into a solid rock.

And may it stand till time shall cease,
    The idol of our country's youth;
As firm as Justice—fair as Peace;
    As beautiful as Truth.

Old soldiers! you may boast to be
    Some of the hope forlorn that hurl'd

The haughty tyrant of the sea
    Off from the western world.

And he is now supremely blest,
    Who on the field of battle still
Can show its scars upon his breast,
    Or tell of Bunker's Hill.

Or of that dark and wintry night,
    When Providence was pleased to bear
The army safely in its flight
    Across the Delaware.

Beneath the flag of stripes and stars,
    What deeds of valor have been done!
Among the free-born sons of Mars,
    It stood by Washington;

"A pillar of a cloud by day,
    A pillar of fire throughout the night;"
The solace of the weary way,
    The spirit of the fight.

Our tree was planted by the sword,
    'T is nurtured by the plough and spade;
And nations now, of one accord,
    Rejoice beneath its shade.

And hoary warriors, while ye stay
    Among us, it shall be our aim
To manifest a will to pay
    The debt ye well may claim.

And to the graves of Freedom's band
    The striplings of our sons shall bring
The future daughters of the land,
    To strew the flowers of Spring.

THE EGYPTIAN GIRL'S SONG.

BY MRS. SARAH J. HOWE.

Bend softly down, ye gentle skies,
    Bend softly down to me;
That I may see those spirit-eyes,
    If spirit-eyes they be—
Bend gently down, for I have dream'd
    That there were forms above
In every pearly star that beamed,
    Made up of light and love.

Bend softly down, ye gentle stars,
    And lift the azure veil,
That I may see your pearly brows
    That ne'er with sorrow pale.
There must be hearts in that blue realm
    That throb with fearful bliss,
They cannot be so dull and cold,
    So pulseless as in this.

Oh! I have set my weary heart
    On love this earth hath not,
And mine through life must ever be
    A sad and lonely lot.
Bend softly down, ye gentle skies,
    Bend softly down to me;
That I may see those spirit-eyes,
    If spirit-eyes they be!

FALLS OF A FOREST STREAM

BY EPHRAIM PEABODY.

Sundered and riven apart, as if
    By some vast earthquake-shock,
Sheer down and deep on either side,
    Descend the walls of rock;
And fast between the fronting sides,
    From their far forest head,
The waters flow, and flash, and fall
    Over their shelving bed.

Eternally, eternally,
    The ceaseless waters flow,
And o'er the brink of the abyss
    The forests stoop and grow;
And silently and solemnly,
    The yew-tree casts its shade,
And the massive shadows of the oak
    Across the gulf are laid.

Up each steep rock-built parapet
    The moss and lichen cling,
And tender cliff-flowers from each rift
    In timid beauty spring;

And sanctuaried from human feet,
   No sound the ear receives,
Save from the falling waters,
   And the wind-stirred boughs and leaves.

O'er all there broods repose; the breeze
   Lingers as it goes past;
The squirrel's foot sounds loud among
   The leaves by autumn cast;
And the lonely bird, whose glancing wing
   Flits restlessly among
The boughs, stops doubtfully, and checks
   The sudden burst of song.

And silently, year after year
   Is ushered in and goes,
And time, amid these quiet scenes,
   No other measure knows
But the wakening and the sleep of birds,
   The dawn and shut of day,
And the changes of the forest leaves,
   From budding to decay.

The wilderness is still; the long,
   Long sleep of ages gone,
With its unmoving presence, fills
   These distant shades and lone;
And changing dynasties, and thrones
   Cast down, send hither brief

And fainter echoes than the fall
    Of autumn's whithered leaf.

The selfsame rest is here, as when
    The Indian made his bed
Beneath the trees, and the mild stars
    Shone in upon his head;
Or when the stag here sought the cool
    Amid the noonday's heat,
Unstartled by the rifle
    Or the tread of hunter's feet.

It is a holy spot; wide lies
    The unbroken hush of woods,
And green-arched pathways lead away
    Through hermit solitudes;
And ceaselessly, and ceaselessly,
    The sliding stream goes past,
And bending over all the hills
    The sky's blue dome is cast.

And far away from the world's jars,
    The heart looks up to Him,
Whose presence seems more near amid
    The forests vast and dim:
And wilderness, and sky, and earth
    By man unmarred, untrod,
And nature's quiet courses, show
    The image of their God.

But the time comes when this repose
    Shall be disturbed and gone,
When the woodman's axe shall lay
    The valleys open to the sun;
When the old Wilderness shall fall,
    And the unsheltered stream,
In all its windings, find no shade
    From summer's fervent beam.

But still the naked heavens shall rest
    Upon the horizon's verge,
And the hurrying waters o'er their bed
    Their rapid current urge;
And hills and vales lie green, while He
    Who sees the sparrow fall,
Shall shed, with an indulgent love,
    A light and peace o'er all.

JERUSALEM.

BY WILLIAM WALLACE.

Queen of Judea's stricken land,
    Thy garland, faded from thy brow,
Lies withered on the desert's sand
    And trampled by the Arab now.
The laurel boughs of Lebanon
    Still brush the blue unspotted sky;—
Their plumes still quiver in the sun,
    Which lights thy ruins from on high;—
But on thy brow so desolate,
Seems stamped the blasting seal of fate!

Bright Kedron's brook still flows along
    In odors, 'neath the palm tree's shade,
Unmindful of the pilgrim's song,
    Upon its banks there weeping laid;—
And Gethsemene's spicy bowers
    Trail their low vines upon the ground;—
Withered and blasted are its flowers,
    Which once did lull their fragrance round;—
Nought greens the cursed and sterile clod,
Save where perchance the Saviour trod!

But nought upon thy guilt-stained brow
  Will rear its verdant, blooming head!
Nought but the paly meteor's glow
  Lights up the "city of the dead!"
Thou fallen Queen! thy lyre is broke,
  Which thrilled to thy own God alone!
No longer to th' inspired stroke
  Of monarch minstrel on the throne
Its chords of gratitude resound,
Or breathe their hallowed notes around.

Above the sculptured column's form
  The mournful cypress twines in gloom,
Whilst in the glistening sunbeams warm
  The scorpion basks upon the tomb!
The marble hall where music rolled,
  The silent street—the holy dome,
Of thousand spires of gleaming gold,
  Are now the savage jackall's home!
And o'er the temple's sacred shrines,
A wreath of death, the ivy twines.

Far o'er thy brow, Jerusalem,
  Calvary's stained height in vengeance towers:
The blood which dropped from Jesse's stem
  Still reddens Gethsemene's bowers.
But shall the desert's sun no more
  Shed its bright rays round nature's tomb?

Shall not the star which glittered o'er
  The heathen night of blackest gloom,
Again gleam round its emerald light,—
Again dispel Judea's night?

Rise! rise, Imperial Salem, rise!
  Lo! on thee dawns Millennial morn!
Look up! look up, upon the skies!
  See—see, its herald star, new-born,
Hangs o'er thy brow a brilliant token,
That the dread curse's spell is broken!

THE VIOLET.

WRITTEN FOR A LITTLE GIRL TO SPEAK ON MAY-DAY,
IN THE CHARACTER OF THE VIOLET.

BY JAMES F. CLARKE.

When April's warmth unlocks the clod,
  Softened by gentle showers,
The violet pierces through the sod,
  And blossoms, first of flowers;
So may I give my heart to God,
  In childhood's early hours.

Some plants, in gardens only found,
   Are raised with pains and care;
God scatters *violets* all around,
   They blossom everywhere;
Thus may my love to *all* abound,
   And all my fragrance share.

Some scentless flowers stand straight and high,
   With pride and haughtiness;
But violets perfume land and sky,
   Although they promise less.
Let me, with like humility,
   Do more than I profess.

Sweet flower, be thou a type to me,
   Of blameless joy and mirth,
Of widely scattered sympathy,
   Embracing all God's earth—
Of early blooming piety,
   And unpretending worth.

THE MUSQUETOE'S SONG.

BY JAMES W. WARD.

In the dreamy hour of night I'll hie,
When the hum is hushed of the weary fly,
When the lamps are lit and the curtains drawn,
And sport on my wings till the morning dawn.
In the festive hall where all is joy,
In the chambers hushed where the sleepers lie;
In the garden bower where the primrose smiles,
And the chirping cricket the hour beguiles;
   In these I'll sport through the summer night,
   And mortals to vex, I'll bite, I'll bite.

There's one I view with an evil eye:
A flame of pride in his breast I spy;
He breathes in the lute with a master's skill,
And listening souls the rich strains fill
With the rapturous thrill of melody;
But he carries his head so haughtily,
I'll play him a trick; in his happiest swell,
When the lingering trill, with a magic spell,
   Holds all entranced—I'll wing my flight,
   And pop on his nose, and I'll bite, I'll bite.

There 's a poet I know—in the still midnight,
He plies his pen by a taper light;
And wearied of earth, in a world all his own,
With fancy he rambles, where flowers are strown
Of fadeless hue; and he images there
A creation of love in the pure still air.
With the world around from his sense shut out,
He heeds not the buzz of my round-about;
  But when a new image has broke on his sight,
  Ere he give it existence, I'll bite, I'll bite—

And the long courted vision shall vanish; while I
In a snug little corner will watch him so shy,
As he thumps his brow in a burning rage,
And dashes his pen o'er the well filled page.
I see a young maid in her chamber napping,
And I know that love at her heart is tapping;
She dreams of a youth, and smiles in bliss,
As she pouts her lips to receive a kiss.
  But she shall not taste the gentle delight,
  For I'll light on her lips—and I'll bite, I'll bite.

TO MARY.

ON THE FIRST LEAF OF MY COMMON-PLACE BOOK.

BY JAMES B. MARSHALL.

Here, Mary, may'st thou read my thoughts
   When I am far away from thee,
Gather'd like autumn-leaves, that fall
   Upon a waveless sea.

Here may'st thou trace the sunny dream
   That brightened o'er my boyhood's brow,—
Here may'st thou learn whence that dark shade
   Which made me pensive now.

Here may'st thou see the smile of love,
   When rapture woke beneath thy smile;
Here may'st thou mark the blanched cheek—
   Oh! thou wast sad the while.

No ripples o'er the silver lake
   Of hope or sable memory,
But glass with magic skill thy form,—
   My heart is all in thee.

Thou art a mother in my grief,
   A sister in my hours of sadness,
Thou art my child to wean me from
   My sorrow with thy gladness.

Thy smile to me is what the sun's
   Gay radiance to the flowers may be;
Giving them life and health and strength—
   Thou art that sun to me.

Then when thou look'st within this book,
   On every page thou 'lt find how dear
Thou art to me—my every thought
   For thee is treasured here.

MAY.

BY WILLIAM D. GALLAGHER.

Would that thou could'st last for aye,
Merry, ever-merry May!
Made of sun-gleams, shade and showers,
Bursting buds, and breathing flowers;
Dripping-lock'd, and rosy-vested,
Violet-slippered, rainbow-crested;
Girdled with the eglantine,
Festoon'd with the dewy vine:

Merry, ever-merry May,
Would that thou could'st last for aye!

Out beneath thy MORNING sky!
Dian's bow still hangs on high;
And in the blue depths afar,
Glimmers, here and there, a solitary star.
Diamonds robe the bending grass,
    Glistening, early flowers among—
Monad's world, and fairy's glass,
Bathing fount for wandering sprite—
    By mysterious fingers hung,
In the lone and quiet night.
Now the freshening breezes pass—
Gathering, as they steal along,
Rich perfume, and matin song—
And quickly to destruction hurl'd
Is fairy's diamond glass, and monad's dew-drop world.
Lo! yon cloud, which hung but now
Black upon the mountain's brow,
Threatening the green earth with storm—
See! it heaves its giant form,
And, ever changing shape and hue,
Each time presenting something new,
Moves slowly up, and spreading rolls away
Towards the rich purple streaks that usher in the day;
Bright'ning, as it onward goes,
Until its very centre glows
With the warm, cheering light, the coming sun bestows:

As the passing Christian's soul,
Nearing the celestial goal,
Bright and brighter grows, till God illumes the Whole.

Out beneath thy NOONTIDE sky!
On a shady slope I lie,
   Giving fancy ample play;
And there's not more blest than I,
   One of Adam's race to-day.
Out beneath thy noontide sky!
Earth, how beautiful!—how clear
Of cloud or mist the atmosphere!
What a glory greets the eye!
What a calm, or quiet stir,
Steals o'er Nature's worshipper—
Silent, yet so eloquent,
That we feel 't is heaven-sent—
Waking thoughts that long have slumber'd
Passion-dimm'd and earth-encumber'd—
Bearing soul and sense away,
To revel in the Perfect Day
Which 'waits us, when we shall for aye
Discard this darksome dust—this prison-house of clay!

Out beneath thy EVENING sky!
Not a breeze that wanders by
But hath swept the green earth's bosom—
Rifling the rich grape-vine blossom,

Dallying with the simplest flower
In mossy nook and rosy bower—
To the perfum'd green-house straying,
And with rich exotics playing—
Then, unsated, sweeping over
Banks of thyme, and fields of clover!
Out beneath thy evening sky!
Groups of children caper by,
Crown'd with flowers, and rush along
With joyous laugh, and shout, and song.
Flashing eye, and radiant cheek,
Spirits all unsunn'd bespeak.
They are in Life's May-month hours—
And those wild bursts of joy, what are they but Life's
  flowers?

Would that thou could'st last for aye,
Merry, ever-merry May!
Made of sun-gleams, shade and showers,
Bursting buds, and breathing flowers;
Dripping-lock'd, and rosy-vested,
Violet-slippered, rainbow-crested;
Girdled with the eglantine,
Festoon'd with the dewy vine:
Merry, ever-merry May,
Would that thou could'st last for aye!

WEDDED LOVE.

BY MRS. ANNE P. DINNIES.

Come, rouse thee, dearest!—'t is not well
    To let the spirit brood
Thus darkly o'er the cares that swell
    Life's current to a flood.
As brooks, and torrents, rivers, all,
Increase the gulf in which they fall,
Such thoughts, by gathering up the rills
Of lesser griefs, spread real ills;
And, with their gloomy shades, conceal
The land-marks Hope would else reveal.

Come, rouse thee, now—I know thy mind,
    And would its strength awaken;
Proud, gifted, noble, ardent, kind—
    Strange thou shouldst be thus shaken!
But rouse afresh each energy,
And be what heaven intended thee;
Throw from thy thoughts this wearying weight,
And prove thy spirit firmly great:
I would not see thee bend below
The angry storms of earthly wo.

Full well I know the generous soul
    Which warms thee into life,
Each spring which can its powers control,
    Familiar to thy Wife—
For deemest thou she had stooped to bind
Her fate unto a *common mind?*
The eagle-like ambition, nursed
From childhood in her heart, had first
Consumed, with its Promethean flame,
The shrine that sunk her so to shame.

Then rouse thee, dearest, from the dream
    That fetters now thy powers:
Shake off this gloom—Hope sheds a beam
    To gild each cloud that lowers;
And though at present seems so far
The wished-for goal—a guiding star,
With peaceful ray, would light thee on,
Until its utmost bounds be won:
That quenchless ray thou 'lt ever prove,
In fond, undying, *Wedded Love.*

MUSINGS.

BY MRS. REBECCA S. NICHOLS.

How like a conqueror the King of Day
    Folds back the curtains of his orient couch!
Bestrides the fleecy clouds, and speeds his way
    'Mid skies made brighter by his burning touch;
And as a warrior from the tented field,
    Victorious, hastes his wearied limbs to rest,
So doth the Sun his brazen sceptre yield,
    And sink, fair Night, upon thy gentle breast.

All hail, sad Vesper! on thy girdled throne
    Thou sit'st a queen, O twilight watcher-star;
How oft I find me gazing towards thy home,
    Pale, dreamy dweller of the realms afar;
And when at eve's most holy, chastened hour,
    I watch each lesser star within its shrine,
How do I miss the strange, mysterious power,
    That chains my spirit to thine orb divine.

Fair Vesper! when thy golden tresses gleam
    Amid the banners of the sunset sky,
Thy spirit floats on every radiant beam,
    Gilding with beauty thy proud place on high;
Then hath my soul its hour of deepest bliss,
    And gentle thoughts like angels round me throng,

Breathing of worlds, (oh! how unlike to this!)
   Where dwell eternal melody and song.

Star of the twilight! thou wert loved by *one*,
   Whose spirit late hath passed away from earth;
Who parted from us, when the wailing tone
   Of some lone winds told of pale autumn's birth;
Yet, though we miss her at the eventide,
   And eyes gaze sadly on the vacant chair,
Though from the hearth her music-tones have died,
   And gone glad laughter that resounded there;

Still from her high and holy place above,
   None would recall her to this earthly sphere,
Nor seek to win her from that home of love,
   To tread the paths of sin and sorrow here.
But lo! clouds gather round fair Cynthia's home,
   And fling their draperies on the arching skies,
Whilst, one by one, depart from yon vast dome,
   The blue sky's many bright and burning eyes.

And she, pale spirit of the midnight skies,
   Whose tears of light were streaming o'er the heath,
Now seems unto my wakeful, watching eyes,
   Like some lone weeper in the house of death!
The storm hath burst—the lightning's angry eye
   Glances around me, and the hoarse winds tell
The raging tempest's might and majesty;
   Bright thoughts have vanished—gentle star, *farewell!*

THE GREEN HILLS OF MY FATHER-LAND.

BY MRS. LAURA M. THURSTON.

The green hills of my father-land
   In dreams still greet my view;
I see once more the wave-girt strand—
   The ocean-depth of blue—
The sky—the glorious sky, outspread
   Above their calm repose—
The river, o'er its rocky bed
   Still singing as it flows—
The stillness of the Sabbath hours,
   When men go up to pray—
The sun light resting on the flowers—
The birds that sing among the bowers,
   Through all the summer-day.

Land of my birth!—mine early love!
   Once more thine airs I breathe!
I see thy proud hills tower above—
   Thy green vales sleep beneath—
Thy groves, thy rocks, thy murmuring rills,
   All rise before mine eyes,
The dawn of morning on thy hills,
   Thy gorgeous sunset skies,—

Thy forests, from whose deep recess
　　A thousand streams have birth,
Glad'ning the lonely wilderness,
And filling the green silentness
　　With melody and mirth.

I wonder if my home would seem
　　As lovely as of yore!
I wonder if the mountain stream
　　Goes singing by the door!
And if the flowers still bloom as fair,
　　And if the woodbines climb,
As when I used to train them there,
　　In the dear olden time!
I wonder if the birds still sing
　　Upon the garden tree,
As sweetly as in that sweet spring
Whose golden memories gently bring
　　So many dreams to me!

I know that there hath been a change,
　　A change o'er hall and hearth!
Faces and footsteps new and strange,
　　About my place of birth!
The heavens above are still as bright
　　As in the days gone by,
But vanished is the beacon light
　　That cheered my morning sky!

And hill, and vale, and wooded glen,
    And rock, and murmuring stream,
That wore such glorious beauty then,
Would seem, should I return again,
    The record of a dream!

I mourn not for my childhood's hours,
    Since, in the far-off West,
'Neath sunnier skies, in greener bowers,
    My heart hath found its rest.
I mourn not for the hills and streams
    That chained my steps so long,
Yet still I see them in my dreams,
    And hail them in my song;
And often by the hearth-fire's blaze,
    When winter eves shall come,
We'll sit and talk of other days,
And sing the well-remembered lays
    Of my green mountain home.

MY SISTERS.

BY MRS. AMELIA B. WELBY.

LIKE flowers that softly bloom together,
    Upon one fair and fragile stem,
Mingling their sweets in sunny weather,
    Ere strange rude hands have parted them:
So were we linked unto each other,
    Sweet Sisters! in our childish hours,
For then one fond and gentle Mother
    To us was like the stem to flowers.
She was the golden thread that bound us
    In one bright chain together here,
Till Death unloosed the cord around us,
    And we were severed far and near.

The floweret's stem, when broke or shattered,
    Must cast its blossoms to the wind,
Yet round the buds, though widely scattered,
    The same soft perfume still we find;
And thus, although the tie is broken
    That linked us round our mother's knee,
The memory of words we've spoken
    When we were children light and free,
Will, like the perfume of each blossom,
    Live in our hearts where'er we roam,

As when we slept on one fond bosom,
    And dwelt within one happy home.

I know that changes have come o'er us:
    Sweet Sisters! we are not the same,
For different paths now lie before us,
    And all three have a different name;
And yet, if Sorrow's dimming fingers
    Have shadowed o'er each youthful brow,
So much of light around them lingers,
    I cannot trace those shadows now.
Ye both have those who love ye only,
    Whose dearest hopes are round ye thrown—
While, like a stream that wanders lonely,
    Am I, the youngest, wildest one.

My heart is like the wind that beareth
    Sweet scents upon its unseen wing—
The wind! that for no creature careth,
    Yet stealeth sweets from every thing;
It hath rich thoughts forever leaping
    Up, like the waves of flashing seas,
That with their music still are keeping
    Soft time with every fitful breeze;
Each leaf that in the bright air quivers,
    The sounds from hidden solitudes,
And the deep flow of far-off rivers,
    And the loud rush of many floods:

All these, and more, stir in my bosom
    Feelings that make my spirit glad,
Like dew-drops shaken in a blossom;
    And yet there is a something sad
Mixed with those thoughts, like clouds, that hover
    Above us in the quiet air,
Veiling the moon's pale beauty over
    Like a dark spirit brooding there.

But, Sisters! those wild thoughts were never
    Yours, for ye would not love like me
To gaze upon the stars forever,
    To hear the wind's wild melody.
Ye 'd rather look on smiling faces,
    And linger round a cheerful hearth,
Than mark the stars' bright hiding places
    As they peep out upon the earth.
But, Sisters! as the stars of even
    Shrink from day's golden flashing eye,
And, melting in the depths of heaven,
    Veil their soft beams within the sky:
So will we pass, the joyous-hearted,
    The fond, the young, like stars that wane,
Till every link of earth be parted,
    To form in heaven *one mystic chain*.

A RHYME OF MAY MORNING.

BY WILLIAM D. GALLAGHER.

MAY-MORNING! May-morning!—The bird from its bough,
And the maid from her chamber, are hurrying now;
That glad in its heart at the coming of day,
And she to go maying, through woodlands away.
The lark with the dawn shakes the dew from his wings,
And aloft from the meadow exultingly springs;
And frequent, though distant he be, ye may hear
Reveillé shrilly sounded by proud chanticleer.

May-morning! May-morning!—Thy breath stirreth now
The dark curls on many a beautiful brow;
And from fairy-like forms, as they hasten along,
Burst gushings of gladness and snatches of song.
The dew-drops that hang on the glittering grass,
Flash brightly and dance in their way as they pass;
And each bird, as it swings on its high, airy stem,
Carols sweetly its liveliest notes for them.

May-morning! May-morning!—Song, laughter and shout,
'Mid thy bushes and blossoms ring joyously out;
For hearts yet untouch'd by the canker of care,
And shadowless spirits, unfetter'd, are there.

And white hands are gath'ring, in wreath and bouquet,
Fresh flow'rs for the bow'r on the hill-side to-day,
Where, 'neath the calm sky, 'mid the spring's smiling green,
The loyal and fair crown their merry May-Queen.

THE PRINCESS PAULINE TO THE PORTRAIT OF NAPOLEON.

BY OTWAY CURRY.

" She died soon after, still calm and mistress of herself, except that in her last hour of agony, she often spoke in so low a tone that she could not be heard distinctly ; but her dying eye, steadfastly fixed upon her brother's portrait, showed clearly that her spirit was holding converse with him———"

ONE hope in all this weary life,
   One living, only joy, was mine ;
With thee above its stormy strife
   To rise, and reign, and shine—
To bless thee when thy kingly name
Was blended with undying fame.

But now alike in ruin lie
   Thy crowns, and thy imperial throne ;
And thou hast journeyed far on high,
   Into that world unknown,

Which lies beyond those orbs of light
That greet us in the lonely night.

And I, alas! when thou art gone,
  With the sweet music of thy voice,
I weep, and there remaineth none
  To bid my heart rejoice:
Oh, for that music's matchless power,
To soothe me in this gloomy hour.

I feel the heavy hand of fate
  Impel me to the eternal shore—
I fear the grave, so desolate
  And dark, that lies before:
Oh! whisper me where thou art gone,
And cheer my drooping spirit on.

Ev'n now I meet thy flashing eye!
  I feel its spirit-thrilling glance.
Oh! let me hear thy battle-cry,
  My brother, "Charge for France!"
Alas for thee, Napoleon!
Alas for France when thou art gone.

TO A CHILD.

BY JAMES H. PERKINS.

My little friend, I love to trace
Those lines of laughter on thy face,
Which seems to be the dwelling place
   Of all that 's sweet :
And bend with pride to thy embrace
   Whene'er we meet.

For though the beauty of the flower,
Or of the sky at sunset hour,
Or when the threat'ning tempests lower,
   May be divine,
Yet unto me but weak their power
   Compared with thine.

And though the ocean waves, which roll
From the equator to the pole,
May tell us of a God's control,
   Yet poor they be,
When measur'd by the living soul
   Which burns in thee.

Of vast, strange cities we are told,
That were in the dim days of old ;

Of thrones of ivory and gold,
        By jewels hid;
And temples of gigantic mould,
        And pyramid:

But I would brave a hundred toils
To watch thy little ways and wiles,
And bathe my spirit in thy smiles,
        And hear thy call,
Rather than walk a dozen miles
        To see them all.

For thou, when folly hath beguiled,
Or selfishness, or sense defiled,
Thou meetest me, my little child,
        Fresh with my stain—
But when upon me thou hast smiled,
        I 'm pure again.

Oh, then, by thee I could be led
With joy life's humblest walk to tread:
The lowliest roof, the hardest bed,
        Were all I 'd ask;
To raise my heart above my head
        Should be my task.

What then to me the diamond stone?
And what the gem-encircled zone?

And what the harp's bewitching tone?
    Thine azure eye,
Thy ruddy cheek, and laugh, alone,
    Would satisfy.

And though all fortune were denied
I 'd struggle still against the tide,
Nor pray for any wealth beside,
    If I could be
The parent, governor, and guide
    Of one like thee

YOUTH'S VISION OF THE FUTURE.

BY THOMAS H. SHREVE.

Before we hear the mournful chime
 Of Sadness falling on the hours,
Before we feel the winds of Time
 Like frost-breath on the heart's wild flowers,—

We stand by Life's mysterious stream,
 Viewing the stars reflected there;
And dream not that each vivid gleam
 Can ever be o'ercast by care.

But as its murmurs gently rise,
    The lute's soft magic haunts each tone;—
We hear not stricken hearts' sad sighs,
    Or dark-browed Grief's unwelcome moan.

Like some weird sybil, Fancy, then.
    The Future's tale breathes on the heart,
Conjuring up heroic men
    And women acting angels' part.

And Hope, like some wild artist, too,
    Sketches Life's scenery to the eye,
Where, spell-bound by each dazzling view,
    We see no sorrowing forms pass by.

That fair and gentle siren, Love,
    Breathes her sweet tones upon the wind,
And glorious women graceful move
    Before us, beautiful and kind:

Fame whispers to the eager ear
    Of mighty triumphs to be won,
Of laurels which no time shall sear,
    And banners flaunting in the sun.

She points us to the lordly few
    Whose brows no shades oblivious wear,—
Entranced by them, we do not view
    The ghosts of thousands inurned there.

Thus dreams the enthusiast youth, who stands
    Beside Life's dark, mysterious stream,
And gazes on the fairy lands
    Which brightly on his vision beam.

Like mirage on the desert's wastes
    His future in the distance smiles;
And onward as he eager hastes,
    It still deceives him and beguiles.

Or like those islands ever green
    Amid the ocean's heaving main,
Which dreaming mariners have seen,
    But which no eye hath seen again.

Life is not formed of flattering dreams,
    But duties which rouse up the soul,
While, here and there, there shoot star-gleams
    To light the laborer to his goal.

THE FREED BIRD.

BY MRS. AMELIA B. WELBY.

Thy cage is open'd, bird! too well I love thee
   To bar the sunny things of earth from thee;
A whole broad heaven of blue lies calm above thee,
   The greenwood waves beneath, and thou art free—
These slender wires shall prison thee no more—
Up, bird! and 'mid the clouds thy thrilling music pour.

Away! away! the laughing waters playing
   Break on the fragrant shore in ripples blue,
And the green leaves unto the breeze are laying
   Their shining edges fringed with drops of dew—
And here and there a wild-flower lifts its head,
Refreshed with sudden life, from many a sunbeam shed.

How sweet thy voice will sound! for o'er yon river
   The wing of Silence like a dream is laid,
And nought is heard save where the wood-boughs quiver,
   Making rich spots of trembling light and shade—
And a new rapture thy wild spirit fills,
For joy is on the breeze, and morn upon the hills.

Now, like the aspen, plays each quivering feather
   Of thy swift pinion bearing thee along,

Up, where the morning stars once sang together,
    To pour the fullness of thine own rich song;
And now thou'rt mirrored to my dazzled view,
A little dusky speck, amid a world of blue.

Yet I will shade mine eye, and still pursue thee
    As thou dost melt in soft ethereal air,
Till angel-ones, sweet bird, will bend to view thee,
    And cease their hymns awhile thine own to share;
And there thou art, with white clouds round thee furled,
Just poised beneath yon vault that arches o'er the world.

A free wild spirit unto thee is given,
    Bright minstrel of the blue celestial dome!
For thou wilt wander to yon upper heaven,
    And bathe thy plumage in the sunbeam's home;
And soaring upward from thy dizzy height,
On free and fearless wing, be lost to human sight.

Lute of the summer clouds! whilst thou art singing
    Unto thy Maker thy soft matin hymn,
My own wild spirit, from its temple springing,
    Would freely join thee in the distance dim;
But I can only gaze on thee, and sigh,
With heart upon my lip—bright minstrel of the sky!

And yet, sweet bird! bright thoughts to me are given,
    As many as the clustering leaves of June,

And my young heart is like a harp of heaven
　　Forever strung unto some pleasant tune;
And my soul burns with wild poetic fire,
Though simple are my strains, and simpler still my lyre.

And now, farewell! the wild wind of the mountain,
　　And the blue streams, alone my strains have heard;
And it is well, for from my heart's deep fountain
　　They flow uncultured as thine own—sweet bird!
For my free thoughts have ever spurned control,
Since this heart held a wish, and this frail form a soul.

BURIAL OF THE BEAUTIFUL.

BY JOHN B. DILLON.

Where shall the dead, and the beautiful, sleep?
In the vale where the willow and cypress weep;
Where the wind of the west breathes its softest sigh;
Where the silvery stream is flowing nigh,
And the pure, clear drops of its rising sprays
　　Glitter like gems in the bright moon's rays—
Where the sun's warm smile may never dispel
Night's tears o'er the form we loved so well—

In the vale where the sparkling waters flow;
Where the fairest, earliest violets grow;
Where the sky and the earth are softly fair,
   Bury her there—bury her there!

Where shall the dead, and the beautiful, sleep?
Where wild flowers bloom in the valley deep;
Where the sweet robes of spring may softly rest,
In purity, over the sleeper's breast:
Where is heard the voice of the sinless dove,
Breathing notes of deep and undying love;
Where no column proud in the sun may glow,
To mock the heart that is resting below;
Where pure hearts are sleeping, forever blest;
Where wandering Perii love to rest;
Where the sky and the earth are softly fair,
   Bury her there—bury her there!

THE OHIO.

BY EPHRAIM PEABODY.

Flow on, thou glorious river,
Thy mountain-shores between,
To where the Mexique's stormy waves
Dash on savannahs green.
Flow on, between the forests
That bend above thy side,
And 'neath the sky and stars, that lie
Mirrored within thy tide.

High in the distant mountains
Thy first small fountains gush,
And down the steep, through the ravine,
In shallow rills they rush;
Till in the level valley,
To which the hills descend,
Converging from the summits, meet
The thousand rills, and blend.—
And soon the narrow mountain stream,
O'er which a child might leap,
Holds on its course with a giant's force,
In a channel broad and deep.

High up among the mountains,
The fisher boy is seen,

Alone and lounging in the shade,
Along the margin green;
And not a sound disturbs him, save
A squirrel or a bird,
Or on the autumn leaves, the noise
" Of dropping nuts is heard."—
But here, the city crowds upon
The freedom of the wave,
And many a happy village bank
Thy flowing waters lave.
Upon thy tranquil bosom, floats
An empire's burdened keels,
And every tributary stream,
An empire's wealth reveals.

Flow on, thou mighty river!
High-road of nations, flow!
And thou *shalt* flow, when all the woods
Upon thy sides, are low.
Yes, thou shalt flow eternally,
Though on thy peopled shore,
The rising town and dawning state
Should sink to rise no more.
Though on the hills were heard no more
A human step or sound,—
Though they were a dead empire's mound,
Still onward shall thy current be,
Thou image of eternity,
Onward and onward to the sea.

THE CLOUDS.

BY CHARLES A. JONES.

The clouds! the clouds! how beautiful
   They move upon the air,
With golden wings dyed in the springs
   Of light the planets bear;
Now onward singly sailing,
   Like eagles, in the breeze,
Then like a gallant gathering
   Of ships upon the seas.

How glorious are their changes!
   Now in pyramids they rise,
And, masses piled on masses,
   They tower to the skies:
Now rising like the glaciers,
   Their summits white as snow,
While in the sun's bright blushings
   They beautifully glow.

How terrible! how terrible,
   When, gloomy, thick and dark,
They form their squadrons o'er the sea,
   Above a gallant bark,

And hurl their lightning arrows
　　Deep in the hissing waves,
While 'mid the mountain-barrows
　　The howling tempest raves:

When from their thronged battalions
　　The thunders wildly sweep,
And from the summits of the waves
　　The shrieking echoes leap;
And mounting on the tempest's wings,
　　The billows lash the sky,
As if the fiends of storm and wave
　　Their battles waged on high.

How beautiful their changes,
　　Like visions in a dream,
When on their rugged surfaces
　　The moon's bright glories gleam;
When wooed by gentle zephyrs,
　　In silver flakes they glide,
Like flocks of sea-gulls sporting
　　Upon the wave in pride.

Now forming into castles,
　　With battlements and moats,
While from the towering turrets
　　A crimson banner floats;
Then as the gentle breeze comes by,
　　The fabric melts away,

And takes the form of legions
    In battle's stern array.

I love those storm-girt wanderers,
    In darkness and in gloom,
When, curtained o'er the vaulted sky,
    Their thunders shake its dome;
I love them, when their brightness
    Is borrowed of the sun.
When as the day departeth,
    The twilight blush comes on.

But still more do I love them
    For the gentle rains they bring,
That summon into life and bloom
    The buds and flowers of spring;
And clothe the vales and mountains
    With robes of living green;
And bid the sparkling fountains
    Whisper joy to every scene.

THE MOUNTAIN PATHS.

BY WILLIAM D. GALLAGHER.

Come to the hills with me!
Come tread the green and flowery paths, that wind
    'Neath many a stately tree
    That, ages lost, hath lined
These airy summits of our Western Land!
The stars are fading, and the breeze is bland.

Come to the hills with me!
The fresh-lipp'd Morn is breathing glorious life.
    Don thy calash, and flee
    The city's dust and strife:
Leave thy prunelle and silken hose, and take
Calf-skin and worsted!—quick, thy toilet make!

    Here—take the garden's pride:
Thy cheek, like it, will soon be rosy-fair.
    Now for the green hill-side,
    And the pure upland air!
Death floats in every breeze that fans us here.
Ready? In sooth thou *look'st* the mountaineer!

    So—we are winding up;
The fair stars have not all yet left the sky:
    There—pluck that honey-cup!
    Thy slender hand will vie

With it in whiteness; and—but I forget—
Dark eyes compare not with the violet:

    Still, pluck it too; I'll call
Thine bright as any star, in any place.
      Nay—let thy bonnet fall
      Back from thy radiant face,
And the fresh breezes with thy ringlets play!—
Whither thine eyes now? Ah! the King of Day!

    Gloriously comes he there!
Morn on the hills! One hour of life like this,
      Pays for whole weeks of care;
      Earth scarce hath greater bliss:
Yet 'angel visits' are almost as many
As visits to the hills—*They turn no penny!*

    What life is this I feel!
A new sensation thrills through every vein:
      And glowing fancies steal
      Athwart my wondering brain:
Visions of Eld—hopes—aspirations—fears
That vanish soon—bright dreams of coming years!

    'Neath these old oaks and elms,
The spirit hath a fullness of delight—
      A depth of joy, that whelms,
      Like the lone, starry night,
Our intellectual being, in a maze,
Where fancy, pleas'd, bewilder'd, startled, plays—

Now floundering in gloom ;
Now reveling in glory, as a ray
The darkness doth illume :
Then bursts the perfect day,
And the clear'd vision wanders wide and free
Through the starred regions of Infinity.

Morn on the hill-tops ! Hark !
The low of kine swells up from yon green vale,
With song of meadow-lark,
And merry note of quail ;
And from each tree-top, by the free wind stirr'd,
Floats the rich matin of some grateful bird.

The breeze is rising now ;
The purple clouds sail gracefully along ;
The spiral saplings bow,
And swell the choral song.
Oh, for the soul to truth and freedom born,
What beauty and what glory hath the Morn !

Yet man alone, of all
To whom Earth's visible blessings have been given,
Deemeth the privilege small
Thus to commune with Heaven :
There is no bank or railroad stock on high—
Stars are not gold—pence rain not from the sky !

MY LOCUST TREE.

BY GEO. B. WALLIS.

My bonnie tree—my bonnie tree,
   Ten years have rolled around,
Since thou wert sent to ornament
   This consecrated ground.
And then thou wert a little twig,
   And I a little wight;
And merrily and cheerily,
   From morning until night,
I gamboll'd 'neath thy narrow screen,
Extending now o'er all the green.

That happy day has passed away,
   Yet 't is in Memory's store
When I transplanted thee, my tree,
   By our grandfather's door:
The clouds in fleet, appeared to meet
   Around the glowing west,
And ruddily and prettily,
   Old Phœbus sank to rest;
And Night had lit her grand saloon,
When I received my picayune.

I planted thee, my bonnie tree,
   In a deep and fertile mould,

And it was fun, when March had gone,
    To see thy buds unfold.
And as the Spring would gently bring
    Their beauties to the light,
Deliciously, propitiously,
    They open'd to the sight;
And thou wert beauteous to be seen,
Array'd in living white and green.

The birds, I thought, that yearly wrought
    Their nest among thy boughs,
Sang their sweet hymns among thy limbs,
    To win me to repose;
And from their throats the mellow notes
    Stole on the passer-by,
Both witchingly and touchingly,
    Like music from the sky.
But, hist! even now I think I hear
That music stealing in my ear.

My bonnie tree, my bonnie tree,
    Our loved ones all are gone,
Who with me play'd beneath thy shade,
    And I am left alone.
I reck not when I may again
    Commingle with the earth:
Fate, viciously, maliciously,
    Has chased me from my birth.
But live, my tree, and wither'd be
The arm upheld to injure thee.

ON JUDAH'S HILLS.

BY HARVEY D. LITTLE.

On Judah's hill the towering palm
   Still spreads its branches to the sky,
The same through years of storm and calm,
   As erst it was in days gone by,
When Israel's king poured forth his psalm
   In strains of sacred melody.

And Lebanon, thy forests green
   Are waving in the lonely wind,
To mark the solitary scene,
   Where wandering Israel's hopes are shrined;
But the famed Temple's ancient sheen
   The pilgrim seeks, in vain, to find.

And Kedron's brook, and Jordan's tide,
   Roll onward to the sluggish sea:
But where is Salem's swollen pride,
   Her chariots, and her chivalry,
Her Tyrian robes in purple dyed,
   Her warlike hosts, who scorned to flee?

Gone! all are gone! In sullen mood
   The cruel Arab wanders there,

In search of human spoils and blood;
   The victims of his wily snare:
And where the holy prophets stood
   The wild beasts make their secret lair.

But, oh! Judea, there shall come
   For thee another glorious morn;
When thy retreats shall be a home
   For thousands pining now forlorn
In distant lands;—no more to roam
   The objects of disdain and scorn.

THE KANAWHA.

WRITTEN AT THE "HAWK'S NEST," A CELEBRATED CLIFF.

BY LEWIS RINGE.

Nature's lover, pause to see,
Where Kanawha wanders free;
Nature in her wildest mood,
'Mid her grandest solitude:
With her mountains thronged around,
Listening to the torrent's sound:
Hill and valley, rock and floods,
Waving with eternal woods:

Here the earth-cloud lowly creeping,
There along the summit sleeping:
Here the cliff uplifting high
Its bold forehead to the sky,
There, like a gigantic lover,
Bending with devotion over
The coy river, swift and clear,—
A gay, bounding mountaineer.
Now it winds away, away,
Sporting with its jewelled spray;
Now it seems to woo your feet,
But, ah! trust not the deceit;
Shrub and pebble though they seem,
Rock and forest guard the stream.
E'en the Grecian lover's leap
Never tempted such a steep,
Where the hawkling far below,
Nestles 'neath the beetling brow;
While along yon craggy bed
Lurks the vengeful copperhead,
And the avalanche of rock
Poises for an earthquake-shock.
All is fresh, sublime, and wild,
As when first by Nature piled,
Ere the white-man wandered here,
Or the red-man chased the deer—
Naming, ere he fled forever,
This, his own Romantic River.

"MY BEAUTIFUL!—MY OWN!"

BY LEWIS J. CIST.

My gentle girl! my loved—my own!
    Whate'er in life betide—
To me come weal or wo, the fates
    I'll mock at and deride.
I would not care, at me were all
    Their shafts of malice thrown,
So long as thee, dear girl, I call
    "MY BEAUTIFUL! MY OWN!"

There may be maidens, love, on earth,
    More fair than even thou;
And noble dames, of loftier birth
    Than thine, there are, I trow;—
But yet, my own dear girl! above
    The queen upon the throne
I prize thee, and thy gentle love—
    "MY BEAUTIFUL! MY OWN!"

There may be those of higher state
    And riches than are thine;
It might be, though thy wealth were great,
    That greater far were mine;
But who could richer treasures find,
    More priceless gems be shown,

Than thine,—the jewels of the mind!—
"My beautiful! my own!"

There may be those more deeply skill'd
   Than thou in musty lore;
There may be heads e'en better fill'd
   With useful learning's store.
Yet learned enough for me thou art;
   Nor learning hast alone,
But a warm, and true, and gushing heart,
   "My beautiful! my own!"

There may be those by *others* deemed
   More beautiful than thou;
But none to *me* have ever seemed
   So worthy Love's pure vow:
Though many a form, with beauty warm
   And loveliest face I 've known,
Yet none to me, but *thou*, can'st be
   "My beautiful! my own!"

"WHEN SHINES THE STAR."

BY MRS. AMELIA B. WELBY.

When shines the star, by thee loved best,
    Upon these soft delicious eves,
Lighting the ring-dove to her nest,
    Where trembling stir the darkling leaves;
When flings the wave its crest of foam
    Above the shadowy-mantled seas,
A softness o'er my heart doth come,
    Linking thy memory with these;
For if, amid those orbs that roll,
    Thou hast at times a thought of me,
For every one that stirs thy soul
    A thousand stir my own of thee.

Even now thy dear remembered eyes,
    Fill'd up with floods of radiant light,
Seem bending from the twilight skies,
    Outshining all the stars of night:
And thy young face divinely fair,
    Like a bright cloud, seems melting through,
While low sweet whispers fill the air,
    Making my own lips whisper too;
For never does the soft south wind
    Steal o'er the hushed and lonely sea,

But it awakens in my mind
    A thousand memories of thee.

Oh! could I,—while these hours of dreams
    Are gathering o'er the silent hills,
While every breeze a minstrel seems
    And every leaf a heart that thrills,—
Steal all unseen to some hush'd place,
    And, kneeling 'neath those burning orbs,
Forever gaze on thy sweet face
    Till seeing every sense absorbs,
And, singling out each blessed even
    The star that earliest lights the sea,
Forget another shines in heaven
    While shines the one beloved by thee.

Lost one! companion of the blest!
    Thou, who in purer air dost dwell,
Ere froze the life-drops in thy breast,
    Or fled thy soul its mystic cell,
We past on earth such hours of bliss
    As none but kindred hearts can know,
And, happy in a world like this,
    But dreamed of that to which we go,
Till thou wast called in thy young years
    To wander o'er that shoreless sea,
Where, like a mist, time disappears,
    Melting into eternity.

I 'm thinking of some sunny hours,
    That shone out goldenly in June,
When birds were singing 'mong the flowers
    With wild sweet voices all in tune,
When o'er thy locks of paly gold
    Flowed thy transparent veil away,
Till 'neath each snow-white trembling fold
    The Eden of thy bosom lay;
And sheltered 'neath its dark-fringed lid
    Till raised from thence in girlish glee,
How modestly thy glance lay hid
    From the fond glances bent on thee.

There are some hours that pass so soon,
    Our spell-touched hearts scarce know they end;
And so it was with that sweet June,
    Ere thou wast lost, my gentle friend!
Oh! how I 'll watch each flower that closes
    Through autumn's soft and breezy reign,
Till summer-blooms restore the roses,
    And merry June shall come again!
But, ah! while float its sunny hours
    O'er fragrant shore and trembling sea,
Missing thy face among the flowers,
    How my full heart will mourn for thee!

A SUMMER SCENE.

BY WILLIAM D. GALLAGHER.

The day was well nigh o'er;
The sun, near the horizon, dimly shone;
And the long shadows of the trees, before
My grassy couch were thrown.
The scene was one I 'd witnessed, many a time,
In the green summer of my boyhood's prime;
And now, in early manhood's ripening day,
Drunk with its beauty, in its heart I lay;
Striving, with necromantic art, to cast
The courses of Life's future from its past;
Then questioning Reason of the spirit's birth,
Essence, and union with this moulded earth;
Anon up-borne, on Fancy's airy pinions,
Far from this world's turmoil, and sordid man's dominions.

Suddenly on my ear,
Rang, full and deep,
Joyous, and musical, and clear,
A sound, which made my father-heart to leap,
And sent the quick blood to my cheek and brow,
Which with the recollection warm e'en now.
Soon ceased the thrilling tone;
And with it pass'd my wild and dreamy train

Of thought—and in the deepening shade again
I lay alone:
So slight a touch can jar the spirit's springs,
And check the boldest flight of Fancy's wandering wings!

Eve came on gently: and her step was seen
Stirring the blossoms on the velvet green,
And warning home the laden bee,
Yet laboring busily.
The while, her soft
And delicate fingers pluck'd the leaves aloft,
And whirled them round and round
In eddies to the ground,
Where I, an humble man, with kingly wreaths was crown'd.

Once more that sweet voice rang upon my ear,
But blent with other sounds, as clear
And musical as it:
A childish jest—and then a shout
From one, or two, or three, rang out,
Full, free, and wild—
And then a fit
Of childish laughter rent the dewy air!
And now my eyes a glimpse caught of the fair
And lovely ONE : it was my own dear child!
She and her little friends, hard at their play,
Upon the grassy slope, that softly stretch'd away.

Again—again—
From the descending plain,
Up rise those gleeful notes: but chief that voice
Which first broke on my ear,
And made my heart rejoice,
Ascends, full, strong, and clear—
Approaching nigh, and nigher,
As the strain grows high, and higher;
Then, like a water-circle, flowing
Away to every point, and growing
Fainter, and fainter, till the last tones die,
Lost, as far-journeying birds fade in the purple sky.

Bonnets were in the air,
And bonnet-ribands scattered on the ground;
Small shoes and pantalettes lay thick around,
And tiny feet were bare;
And frocks were soiled, and aprons rent;
But still they kept their frolic mood,
And laugh'd and romp'd; and when I went
And closer by them stood,
How hard each little elf did try
To win the most of my regard;
Now gazing anxious in my eye,
And striving still more hard;
The spirit, so it seem'd to me,
The same in the great world we see,
Spurring the warrior on to victory,
And urging on the bard:

Each had success as much at heart,
As he who plays in war or politics his part.

"My child!—my child!"
She comes to me:
Her cheeks are flush'd, her hair is wild,
Her pulse is bounding free:
With laugh and shout she comes—but see!
Half way she stops, as still as death;
Her look is sad—she hardly draws a breath.
"My child! my own dear child!
Tell me, what aileth thee?"
"Father!"—she pointed to the moon,
On the horizon's shatter'd bound—
'T was rising, full and round.
"Father! I 'm coming soon."
Her other hand now pointed to the West,
Where the dim sun was sinking to his rest.
"Father! are those the eyes of God
Looking upon us here?"
Her knee bent slowly to the dewy sod—
And then came tear on tear:
A gush of mingled feeling—wonder, and joy, and fear.

SATAN.

BY OTWAY CURRY.

Stern ruler of that lurid clime,
    Along whose vast and gloomy deep
The shadowy winds and hues sublime
    Of never-ending tempests sweep :

Before thy sceptre high and stern
    The armies of the fallen wait
In dark array, and proudly spurn
    The fetters of unchanging fate.

In thy dark home of endless gloom,
    Their warrior legions round thee press,
To meliorate thy fearful doom
    With their unfaltering faithfulness.

Unwavering still, though deadliest ills
    Have worn the smiles all darkly dim
That lured them on the heavenly hills
    To brave the embattled seraphim.

And the bright crown of shining stars,
    That glittered then upon thy brow,
Is changed for deep and fearful scars
    Of everlasting vengeance now.

Oh! thou wast glorious on the hills
   Of Eden in the olden time—
'Mid starry halls, and living rills,
   Unfallen, and unstained with crime.

And glorious, even in fearful strife
   With powers that round the Highest dwell,
When, battling for the thrones of life,
   The arch-angelic leaders fell.

And now beneath thy burning throne
   The stalwart surges fiercely meet,
By spirits of the tempest thrown
   In fiery worship at thy feet.

"LET THERE BE LIGHT."

BY EDWIN R. CAMPBELL.

Darkness was on the mighty deep;
   No light was kindled there;
As yet a drear, unbroken sleep,
   Lay on the sky and air;
Not yet the sun's all quickening ray
Had given to earth the primal day.

No morning light had ever shone
    Upon the new-formed world,
Nor had the evening's starry zone
    Its splendors yet unfurl'd,
To light the dark and trackless waste,
On which His impress had been placed.

"*Let there be light!*"—and as the word
    Came forth o'er earth and sea,
A thousand angel harps were heard
    To sound with melody.
And voices mingled with the chord—
Behold the light—" Praise ye the Lord!"

"*Let there be light!*"—the lightning wove
    Around its dazzling chain,
And from the darkness far above
    Descended on the plain,
And wrote upon the face of night,
In burning words, " Let there be light!"

And light was on the ocean wave,
    And in the dashing spray;
Far in the deep, the glitt'ring cave
    Received the vivid ray,
And many a gem with lustre bright,
Flashed back the word—" Let there be light."

"*Let there be light!*"—the rainbow's hue,
    Where mingle gorgeous dyes,

Far in the vaulted arch of blue
    Is painted on the skies;
Its scroll unfolds to mortal sight—
Behold, oh man! "Let there be light!"

Then praise to Him whose power divine
    Lit up the glitt'ring skies,
Who taught earth's glowing orb to shine
    With light that never dies,
Who from the deep raised earth in air
And set His seal of glory there.

And whilst the stars and planets roll
    Midst Thine eternal spheres,
The lamp that lights the human soul
    A brighter light appears,
And sheds its ray o'er every land
That glows beneath Thy mighty hand.

"*Let there be light!*"—while time remains,
    By power benignest given,
O'er earth's benighted hills and plains—
    The glorious light of heaven,
That breaks through Superstition's gloom,
And sheds a halo round the tomb.

AFTER A STORM.

BY MICAH P. FLINT.

The storm had passed, but not in wrath,
For ruin had not marked its path
O'er that sweet vale, where now was seen
A bluer sky, and brighter green.
There was a milder azure spread
Around the distant mountain's head;
And every hue of that fair bow,
Whose beauteous arch had risen there,
Now sank beneath a brighter glow,
And melted into ambient air.
The tempest, which had just gone by,
Still hung along the eastern sky,
And threatened, as it rolled away.
The birds from every dripping spray,
Were pouring forth their joyous mirth.
The torrent, with its waters brown,
From rock to rock came rushing down;
While, from among the smoking hills,
The voices of a thousand rills
Were heard, exulting at its birth.
A breeze came whispering through the wood,
And, from its thousand tresses, shook
The big round drops, that trembling stood,
Like pearls, in every leafy nook.

AUGUST.

BY WILLIAM D. GALLAGHER.

Dust on thy mantle! dust,
Bright Summer, on thy livery of green!
A tarnish, as of rust,
Dims thy late-brilliant sheen:
And thy young glories—leaf, and bud, and flower—
Change cometh over them with every hour.

Thee hath the August sun
Looked on with hot, and fierce, and brassy face:
And still and lazily run,
Scarce whispering in their pace,
The half-dried rivulets, that lately sent
A shout of gladness up, as on they went.

Flame-like, the long mid-day—
With not so much of sweet air as hath stirr'd
The down upon the spray,
Where rests the panting bird,
Dozing away the hot and tedious noon,
With fitful twitter, sadly out of tune.

Seeds in the sultry air,
And gossamer web-work on the sleeping trees!
    E'en the tall pines, that rear
    Their plumes to catch the breeze,
The slightest breeze from the unfreshening west,
Partake the general languor, and deep rest.

    Happy, as man may be,
Stretch'd on his back, in homely bean-vine bower,
    While the voluptuous bee
    Robs each surrounding flower,
And prattling childhood clambers o'er his breast,
The husbandman enjoys his noon-day rest.

    Against the hazy sky
The thin and fleecy clouds, unmoving, rest.
    Beneath them far, yet high
    In the dim, distant west,
The vulture, scenting thence its carrion-fare,
Sails, slowly circling in the sunny air.

    Soberly, in the shade,
Repose the patient cow, and toil-worn ox;
    Or in the shoal stream wade,
    Sheltered by jutting rocks:
The fleecy flock, fly-scourg'd and restless, rush
Madly from fence to fence, from bush to bush.

Tediously pass the hours,
And vegetation wilts, with blistered root—
And droop the thirsting flow'rs,
Where the slant sunbeams shoot:
But of each tall old tree, the lengthening line,
Slow-creeping eastward, marks the day's decline.

Faster, along the plain,
Moves now the shade, and on the meadow's edge :
The kine are forth again,
The bird flits in the hedge.
Now in the molten west sinks the hot sun.
Welcome, mild eve!—the sultry day is done.

Pleasantly comest thou,
Dew of the evening, to the crisp'd-up grass;
And the curl'd corn-blades bow,
As the light breezes pass,
That their parch'd lips may feel thee, and expand,
Thou sweet reviver of the fevered land.

So, to the thirsting soul,
Cometh the dew of the Almighty's love;
And the scathed heart, made whole,
Turneth in joy above,
To where the spirit freely may expand,
And rove, untrammel'd, in that 'better land.'

LINES TO A LADY.

ON RETURNING TO HER A SPRIG OF CEDAR, WHICH IN FLORAL LANGUAGE MEANS "I LIVE FOR THEE."

BY LEWIS F. THOMAS.

FAIR lady, in those sunny climes
    That lie beneath the eastern skies,
Love's language is not writ in rhymes,
    But beams in looks and breathes in sighs;
And when fond maidens would impart
    To one away, love's magic power,
They send the wishes of the heart
    Interpreted by leaf or flower.
I marked last night thy sigh—thy look—
    Alas! they told no love for me,
Though in this leaf, as in a book,
    I read the words—"I live for thee."

Sweet lady, since thy look or sigh
    Confirms not what this leaflet tells,
O, take it back—nor deem that I
    Think lightly of thy magic spells:
Yes, take it, a memorial still
    Of one who owns thy witching sway,

Whose heart can know no other will
    Than thy fond wishes to obey.
O, keep it—and when hence I fly,
    Let it remind thee oft of me,
And tell, as doth my look and sigh,
    " I live for thee—I live for thee."

PALMYRA.

BY HARVEY D. LITTLE.

How art thou fallen, mighty one!
    Queen of the desert's arid brow!
The evening's shade, the morning's sun,
    Rest only on thy ruins now.
Thine hour is o'er, thy glory done,
    A dreary waste thy charms endow!

In thy proud days thou seem'dst a star,
    Amidst a desert's sullen gloom,
Shedding thy radiance afar
    O'er nature's solitary tomb.
But time, whose gentlest touch can mar,
    Hath sear'd thy tall palmettoe's bloom.

The shouts of joy—the voice of mirth,
   That waked to life thy marble domes:
Thy crowded marts—thy peopled earth—
   Thy sculptur'd halls, and sacred homes,
Are silent now. Thy faded worth
   A barren wilderness entombs.

The savage beast hath made his lair,
   Where pomp and power once held their sway;
And Silence, with a fearful air,
   Sits darkly brooding o'er decay;
And marble fanes, divinely fair,
   Have bowed beneath thine evil day.

Round polish'd shafts the ivy twines
   A wreath funereal for thy fate;
And through thy temples' broken shrines
   The moaning wind sweeps desolate.
But the mild star of evening shines
   Benignly o'er thy fallen state.

Oh, how thy silence chills the heart
   Of the lone traveller, whose tread
Is o'er the fragments of thine art,
   Thou wondrous City of the Dead!
Thy glory cannot yet depart,
   Though all of life hath from thee fled.

THE YOUNG SOLDIER.

BY JAMES H. PERKINS.

> "Now lend the eye a terrible aspect,
> Set firm the teeth, and stretch the nostrils wide,
> Hold hard the breath, and bend up every spirit
> To its full height." *Henry V.*

Oh! was ye ne'er a schoolboy?
And did you never train,
And feel that swelling of the heart
You cannot feel again?
Didst never meet, far down the street,
With plumes and banners gay,
While the kettle, for the kettle-drum
Played your march, march away?

It seems to me but yesterday,
Nor scarce so long ago,
Since we shouldered our muskets
To charge the fearful foe.
Our muskets were of cedar wood,
With ramrod bright and new;
With bayonet forever set,
And painted barrel too.

We charged upon a flock of geese,
And put them all to flight,
Except one sturdy gander
That thought to show us fight:
But, ah! we knew a thing or two;
Our captain wheeled the van—
We routed him, we scouted him,
Nor lost a single man.

Our captain was as brave a lad
As e'er commission bore;
All brightly shone his tin sword,
And a paper cap he wore;
He led us up the hill-side,
Against the western wind,
While the cockerel plume, that decked his head,
Streamed bravely out behind.

We shouldered arms, we carried arms,
We charged the bayonet;
And wo unto the mullen stalk
That in our course we met.
At two o'clock the roll was called,
And till the close of day,
With our brave and plumed captain
We fought the mimic fray,—
When the supper bell, we knew so well,
Came stealing up from out the dell,
For our march, march away.

THE ARMIES OF THE EVE.

BY OTWAY CURRY.

Not in the golden morning
   Shall faded forms return,
For languidly and dimly then
   The lights of memory burn:

Nor when the noon unfoldeth
   Its sunny light and smile,
For these unto their bright repose
   The wondering spirit wile:

But when the stars are wending
   Their radiant way on high,
And gentle winds are whispering back
   The music of the sky—

Oh, then those starry millions
   Their streaming banners weave,
To marshal on their wildering way
   The Armies of the Eve:

The dim and shadowy armies
   Of our unquiet dreams,
Whose footsteps brush the feathery fern
   And print the sleeping streams.

We meet them in the calmness
   Of high and holier climes;
We greet them with the blessed names
   Of old and happier times.

And, marching in the starlight
   Above the sleeping dust,
They freshen all the fountain-springs
   Of our undying trust.

Around our every pathway,
   In beauteous ranks they roam,
To guide us to the dreamy rest
   Of our eternal home.

STANZAS.

BY FREDERIC W. THOMAS.

I 've thought, in many a dreaming hour,
   If I could win the voice of fame—
The wreath without a fading flower,
   That gathers round a glorious name:
That come what might I should be blest,
The gay, the fair, might take the rest.

That woman's smile should but attract,
   Like music at the gorgeous play—
Given between each passing act,
   To wile the tedious time away—
That when the scene employed my care,
I'd heed not how she went, or where.

E'en as the boy who takes the bird,
   And loves to mark its panting breast,
And breathes it many a pretty word,
   And gives it all that birds love best,—
With woman thus I thought to play,
Then, wearied, let her flee away.

That wish for fame, is but a dream,
   Which only in my dreams can live,
And, could I realize the theme,
   What could its frail possession give?
The bird! alas! her notes I've heard—
Oh, that I now could win the bird.

She should my every thought engage—
   'T would be my joy to hear her sing—
And keep her in a willing cage,
   And of my heart I'd make the string,—
Then, Lady-bird, we could not part,
But with a seared and broken heart.

A HARVEST HYMN.

BY WILLIAM D. GALLAGHER.

GREAT GOD!—our heart-felt thanks to Thee!
   We feel thy presence everywhere;
And pray, that we may ever be
   Thus objects of thy guardian care.

We sow'd!—by Thee our work was seen,
   And bless'd; and instantly went forth
Thy mandate; and in living green
   Soon smiled the fair and fruitful earth.

We toil'd!— and Thou didst note our toil;
   And gav'st the sunshine and the rain,
Till ripen'd on the teeming soil
   The fragrant grass, and golden grain.

And now, we reap!—and oh, our God!
   From this, the earth's unbounded floor,
We send our Song of Thanks abroad,
   And pray Thee, bless our hoarded store!

"I KNOW THAT THY SPIRIT."

BY MRS. AMELIA B. WELBY.

I know that thy spirit looks radiantly down
    From yon beautiful orb of the blest,
For a sound and a sign have been set in my own,
    That tell of the place of thy rest;
For I gaze on the star that we talked of so oft,
    As our glances would heavenward rove,
When thy step was on earth, and thy bosom was soft
    With a sense of delight and of love.

The dreams that were laid on thy shadowless brow
    Were pure as a feeling unborn,
And the tone of thy voice was as pleasant and low
    As a bird's in a pleasant spring morn;
Such a heaven of purity dwelt in thy breast,
    Such a world of bright thoughts in thy soul,
That nought could have made thee more lovely or blest,
    So bright was the beautiful whole.

But, now o'er thy breast in the hush of the tomb
    Are folded thy pale graceful arms,
While the midnight of death, like a garment of gloom,
    Hangs over that bosom's young charms;

And pale, pale, alas! is thy rosy lip now,
  Its melody broken and gone,
And cold is the young heart whose sweet dreams below
  Were of summer, of summer alone.

Yet the rise and the fall of thine eye-lids of snow
  O'er their blue orbs so mournfully meek,
And the delicate blush that would vanish and glow
  Through the light of thy transparent cheek,
And thy tresses all put from thy forehead away—
  These, these on my memory rise
As I gaze on yon bright orb whose beautiful ray
  Hath so often been blest by thine eyes.

The blue-girdled stars and the soft dreamy air
  Divide thy fair spirit and mine:
Yet I look in my heart, and a something is there
  That links it in feeling to thine:
The glow of the sunset, the voice of the breeze,
  As it cradles itself on the sea,
Are dear to my bosom, for moments like these
  Are sacred to memory and thee.

AUTUMN MUSINGS.

BY OTWAY CURRY.

'T is Autumn. Many, and many a fleeting age
Hath faded since the primal morn of Time;
And silently the slowly journeying years,
All redolent of countless seasons, pass.

The Spring-time wakes in beauty, and is fraught
With power to thrill the leaping pulse of Joy,
And urge the footsteps of ideal Hope
With flowery lightness on. In peerless day
Resplendent Summer garlandeth the world;
And Contemplation through her sky serene
Ascends unwearied, emulous to lead,
To marshal, and to proudly panoply
The votaries of Ambition as they rise.
These with their gilded pageants disappear,
And vestal Truth leads on the silent hours
Of Autumn's lonely reign. The weary gales
Creep o'er the waters, and the sunbrown plains,
Oft whispering as they pass a long farewell
To the frail emblems of the waning year,
The drooping foliage, and the dying leaves.
This is the time for care; to break the spell
Of ever-fabling Fancy; to contrast

The evanescent beams of earthly bliss
With the long, dread array of deepening ill.
The ills of life are twofold: those which fall
With lead-like weight upon the mortal clay,
Are transient in their kind; for the frail dust
Ere long shall blend with the innumerous sands,
And atoms of the boundless universe,
Absorbed in the unfelt, unconscious rest
Of lifeless, soulless matter, without change,—
Save when the far-off period shall arrive
Of shadowy nothingness.

      The deadlier ills
That tinge existence with unbroken gloom,
Are lost to melioration, for they hold
The ever-during spirit in their grasp,
And in their kind a withering permanence.
To linger in unrest—to be endowed
With high aspirings, endless, limitless!
On Thought's unshackled pinions to outride
The air-borne eagles of the Appenines:
To pierce the surging depths of endless space;
To revel in the stalwart fervidness
Of its careering storms! to sweep sublime
Through the far regions of immensity,
Then fall astounded from the dreaming height,
And wake in wildering durance. These are things
That well may dim the sleepless eyes of care.
And thou, too, Friendship, pilgrim-child of heaven!

The balm that brings the spirit sweet relief
From the keen stings of sorrow and despair,
'T is thine to give : yet the deep quietude
Of the bereaving tomb hath shrouded oft
The morning-prime of beings formed for thee,—
A truth well imaged forth in the sad tale
Of one who mouldereth now in lowly dust.

His soul was fraught with the undying fire
Of seraph Poesy; and he would joy
To cull the flowers from her bright coronal
To gem the brilliant hours. The smiling fields,
The happy homes of men, the verdant plains,
And the lone wilderness, were beauteous all!
And all seemed one vast altar, and the sky
Seemed one vast canopy, the living dome
Of Fame's eternal temple: and the stars,
Her bright, attendant spirits, in his view
Upheld her crowns and garlands. He would climb
The towering cliff, to sit alone and gaze
Upon the wide, blue sea; to hear the mild
Incessant breaking of the murmuring waves—
The endless requiem of the elder world—
And from its billowy chime his spirit drew
Primeval inspiration. Human life
Seemed bland, and beautiful; for on his brow
No breeze had wantoned, save the genial air
Of its unshaded morning. Love had thrown
Its magic round him, and his heart beat high

With rich and pure affection. Happiness
Pervaded all existence; and her smile
Serene, the dreamer fondly deemed would brave
The storms of time forever. Life wore on,
And those bright visions faded, and gave place
To pain and grief:—and he lay down and slept
A long, long sleep:—a sleep, which neither voice
Of youth, nor age, nor childhood's buoyant tread,
Nor Pride's unfaltering footstep in the sheen
Of Manhood's glorious noonday, e'er shall break.
The wintry winds swept round him, but their chill,
Congealing blight the sleeper could not know.
The swiftly changing seasons sped away,
And the bright, burning sunlight flashed upon
His lone, and silent mansion; but its deep,
And gelid gloom, the sunbeam might not gild.

Years followed years away: and when there came
A child of sorrow to his nameless grave,
The waving, rustling grass of deep, bright green,
Was blended with the early, transient bloom
Of Spring's wild blossoms o'er him. She knelt down
And wept, for she had been in by-gone days
The idol of his love; the changed—the lost—
Still almost beautiful, though sorrowing years,
And pain, and sin, had dimm'd her shining brow.

* * * * * * *

And they are resting side by side within
The guileless grave, in death's calm union joined,
Whose bond no storm can sever.

LINES WRITTEN ON THE ROCKY MOUNTAINS.

BY ALBERT PIKE.

The deep, transparent sky, is full
  Of many thousand glittering lights—
Unnumbered stars that calmly rule
  The dark dominions of the night.
The mild bright moon has upward risen,
  Out of the gray and boundless plain,
And all around, the white snows glisten,
  Where frost, and ice, and silence reign,—
While ages roll away, and they unchanged remain.

These mountains, piercing the blue sky
  With their eternal cones of ice;
The torrents dashing from on high,
  O'er rock and crag and precipice;
Change not, but still remain as ever,
  Unwasting, deathless and sublime,
And will remain while lightnings quiver,
  Or stars the hoary summits climb,
Or rolls the thunder-chariot of eternal Time.

It is not so with all—I change,
  And waste as with a living death,

Like one that hath become a strange,
    Unwelcome guest, and lingereth
Among the memories of the past,
    Where he is a forgotten name;
For Time hath greater power to blast
    The hopes, the feelings and the fame,
To make the passions fierce, or their first strength to tame.

    The wind comes rushing swift by me,
        Pouring its coolness on my brow;—
    Such was I once—as proudly free,
        And yet, alas! how altered now!
    Yet while *I* gaze upon yon plain,
        These mountains, this eternal sky,
    The scenes of boyhood come again,
        And pass before the vacant eye,
Still wearing something of their ancient brilliancy.

    Yet why complain?—for what is wrong,
        False friends, cold-heartedness, deceit,
    And life already made too long,
        To one who walks with bleeding feet
    Over its paths?—it will but make
        Death sweeter when it comes at last—
    And though the trampled heart may ache,
        Its agony of pain is past,
And calmness gathers there, while life is ebbing fast.

Perhaps, when I have passed away,
    Like the sad echo of a dream,
There may be some one found to say
    A word that might like sorrow seem.
That I would have—one saddened tear,
    One kindly and regretting thought—
Grant me but that!—and even here,
    Here, in this lone, unpeopled spot,
To breathe away this life of pain, I murmur not.

TO A SEA-SHELL.

BY MRS. AMELIA B. WELBY.

SHELL of the bright sea-waves!
What is it that we hear in thy sad moan?
Is this unceasing music all thine own,
    Lute of the ocean caves!

OR, does some spirit dwell
In the deep windings of thy chamber dim,
Breathing forever, in its mournful hymn,
    Of ocean's anthem swell?

Wert thou a murmurer long
In chrystal palaces beneath the seas,
Ere, on the bright air, thou hadst heard the breeze
    Pour its full tide of song?

Another thing with thee—
Are there not gorgeous cities in the deep,
Buried with flashing gems that darkly sleep,
    Hid by the mighty sea?

And say, oh lone sea-shell,
Are there not costly things, and sweet perfumes
Scattered in waste o'er that sea gulf of tombs?
    Hush thy low moan, and tell.

But yet, and more than all—
Has not each foaming wave in fury tost
O'er earth's most beautiful, the brave, the lost,
    Like a dark funeral pall.?

'T is vain—thou answerest not!
Thou hast no voice to whisper of the dead—
'T is ours alone, with sighs like odors shed,
    To hold them unforgot!

Thine is as sad a strain,
As if the spirit in thy hidden cell
Pined to be with the many things that dwell
    In the wild, restless main.

And yet, there is no sound
Upon the waters, whispered by the waves,
But seemeth like a wail from many graves,
Thrilling the air around.

The earth, oh moaning shell!
The earth hath melodies more sweet than these,
The music-gush of rills, the hum of bees,
Heard in each blossom's bell.

Are not these tones of earth,
The rustling foliage with its shivering leaves,
Sweeter than sounds that e'en in moonlight eves,
Upon the seas have birth?

Alas! thou still wilt moan—
Thou 'rt like the heart that wastes itself in sighs,
E'en when amid bewildering melodies,
If parted from its own.

WHAT IS LIFE?

BY CHARLES D. DRAKE.

An eagle flew up in his heavenward flight,
Far out of the reach of human sight,
And gazed on the earth from his lordly height
   In the clouds of the upper air:
"And this is life," he exultingly screams,
"To soar without fear where the lightning gleams,
And look unblenched on the sun's gorgeous beams,
   And know no harrowing care."

A lion sprang forth from his bloody bed,
And roared till it seemed he would wake the dead;
And man and beast from him trembling fled,
   As though there were death in the tone:
"And this is life," he triumphantly cried,
"To hold my domain in the forest wide,
Imprisoned by nought but the ocean's tide,
   And the ice of the frozen zone."

"It is life," said a whale, "to swim in the deep;
O'er hills submerged and abysses to sweep,
Where the gods of ocean their vigils keep
   In the fathomless gulfs below;

To bask on the bosom of tropical seas,
And inhale the fragrance of Ceylon's breeze;
Or sport where the turbulent waters freeze,
   In the climes of eternal snow."

"It is life," says a tireless albatross,
" To skim through the air, when the black waves toss
In the storm that has swept the earth across,
   And never to wish for rest;
To sleep on the breeze as it softly flies,
My perch in the air, my shelter the skies,
And to build my nest on the billows that rise
   And break with a beautiful crest."

" It is life," said a wild gazelle, " to leap
From crag to crag of the mountain steep,
Where the cloud's icy tears in purity sleep,
   Like the marble brow of death;
To stand, unmoved, on the outermost verge
Of the perilous height, and hear the surge
Of the waters beneath, that onward urge,
   As if sent by a demon's breath."

" It is life," I hear a butterfly say,
" To revel in blooming gardens by day,
And nestle in cups of flowerets gay,
   When the stars the heavens illume;
To steal from the rose its delicate hue,
To sip from the hyacinth glittering dew,

And catch from beds of the violet blue
    The richest and sweetest perfume."

"It is life," a majestic war-horse neighed,
"To prance in the glare of battle and blade,
Where thousands in terrible death are laid,
    And scent of the streaming gore :
To rush unappall'd through the fiery heat,
And trample the dead beneath my feet,
To the trumpet's clang, and the drum's loud beat,
    And hear the artillery roar."

"It is life," said a savage, with hideous yell,
"To roam unshackled the mountain and dell,
And feel my bosom with majesty swell,
    As the primal monarch of all;
To gaze on the earth, the sky, and the sea,
And feel, that, like them, I am chainless and free,
And never, while breathing, to bend the knee,
    But at the Manitou's call."

An aged christian went tottering by,
And white was his hair, and dim was his eye,
And his broken spirit seemed ready to fly,
    As he said, with faltering breath:
"It is life, to move from the heart's first throes,
Through youth and manhood, to age's snows,
In a ceaseless circle of joys and woes :—
    It is life, to prepare for death."

LAKE ERIE.

BY EPHRAIM PEABODY.

These lovely shores! how lone and still
  A hundred years ago,
The unbroken forest stood above,
  The waters dash'd below:—
The waters of a lonely sea,
  Where never sail was furl'd,
Embosomed in a wilderness,
  Which was itself a world.

A hundred years! go back; and lo!
  Where, closing in the view,
Juts out the shore, with rapid oar
  Darts round a frail canoe.—
'T is a white voyager, and see,
  His prow is westward set
O'er the calm wave: hail to thy bold,
  World-seeking bark, Marquette!

The lonely bird, that picks his food
  Where rise the waves, and sink,
At their strange coming, with shrill scream,
  Starts from the sandy brink;
The fishhawk, hanging in mid sky,
  Floats o'er on level wing,

And the savage from his covert looks,
    With arrow on the string.

A hundred years are past and gone,
    And all the rocky coast
Is turreted with shining towns,
    An empire's noble boast.—
And the old wilderness is changed
    To cultured vale and hill;
And the circuit of its mountains
    An empire's numbers fill.

TO EVA: IN HER ALBUM.

BY JAMES B. MARSHALL.

Touch gently with thy taper finger,
    The string of some lov'd lute,—
The cherish'd sound will with thee linger,
    E'en when the string is mute.
And thus I 'd have thy thoughts recur,
    When far away from thee,
To him who leaves a tribute here
    For friendship's memory.

Over the azure sky above,
    Clouds sweep in caravans,
But still the star we watch and love,
    In memory remains;
And even through their dusky forms,
    O'ershadowing earth and sea,
As fiercely driv'n by winter-storms,
    That star is bright to me.

Go grave thy name upon the stone
    O'er which the brooklet hies,
And though with moss it be o'ergrown,
    And hid to duller eyes,
Yet from the eye of love that name
    Can never be effaced,—
Time-covered, 't will as plainly seem
    As though but newly traced.

When starry night doth wane away
    Beneath the sun's gay gleam,
Do we forget the moon's pale ray,
    Lost in a gaudier beam?
Oh with the stars, I 'd have thee keep
    My friendship's memory,
And when I gaze on heaven's blue deep,
    I 'll fondly think of thee.

THE WANDERER'S RETURN.

BY HARVEY D. LITTLE.

I come once more, a wearied man,
    To look upon that holy spot,
Where first my infant life began
    To journey through its changeful lot.
I come!—A thousand shadows play
    Upon the mirror of my mind—
The phantoms of a happier day
    In memory's sacred keeping shrined.

I gaze! and lo! before me rise
    The shades of many a hallowed form:
They pass before my wilder'd eyes,
    With looks as blooming, young, and warm,
As twice ten years ago they seem'd,
    When last in sportive hour we met:
But ah! we then had never dream'd
    That youth's bright sun so soon would set.

Where are they now?—I find them not
    Where erst their glorious forms were found!
Each favorite haunt, each well known spot,
    Echoes no more the cheerful sound

Of their glad voices.—They are gone,
    O'er hills, and streams, and valleys wide;
Scatter'd like leaves by autumn strown,
    Even in their freshest bloom and pride.

The placid brook still winds its way
    Through sloping banks bedeck'd with flowers:
The zephyrs through the leaflets play,
    The same as in life's early hours.
But time and change have strangely cast
    O'er every spot a lonesome air:
My thoughts are treasur'd with the *past*—
    My happiest moments centre there.

I feel that e'en my childhood's home
    Hath lost its once mysterious charm!
No voice parental bids me come—
    None greets me with affection warm!
But yet, amid my being's blight,
    One cherish'd thought with fondness glows—
That where mine eyes first hailed the light,
    There they at *last*, shall darkly close.

LINES TO A POETESS.

BY WILLIAM D. GALLAGHER.

Lady—I know thee only
   Through the breathings of thy song,
But my thought has often pictured thee
   The loveliest of the throng,
Who, in our free, wild forest-land,
   Have knelt them at the shrine
Of Eloquence and Poesy—
   The thrilling, the divine.

The ever-verdant islands
   That dot Mind's soundless sea,
Seem pleasure-walks, and pilgrim-spots,
   Familiar unto thee;
And the flowers of immortal Thought
   That there unfading bloom,
Thou hast their beauty at thy heart,
   Their brightness, their perfume.

Along the blessed Heaven
   Thy spirit holds its way,
In the starry radiance of the night,
   And the golden light of day,—

Its pinions flashing back the sheen
  Of those unclouded spheres,
And its own wild music mingling
  With the angel-notes it hears.

In the human heart already
  Thou hold'st an honored place,
And there thou hast engraven things
  Which nothing can efface.
Hold on, among Earth's gifted, then!
  Tread firm the paths of Fame!
And high, upon the heaven of Mind,
  Thou 'lt write a deathless name.

CHILDHOOD.

BY WILLIAM B. FAIRCHILD.

Oh, beautiful, most beautiful
  Each impulse of the heart,
Ere care hath twined its meshes round
  And planted there its dart—
When youthful blood is coursing through
  Each clear, transparent vein,
With a beauty and a mystery
  That spurn at reason's rein.

Oh, then the " tell-tale countenance"
　　Each thought embodies forth,
And like the gems of night, the eyes
　　Do sparkle, bright with mirth—
And shadowings that flit across
　　The clear and polished brow,
Tell but of feelings in the heart
　　As pure as love's first vow.

No trial of this dark, dark world—
　　No load of fev'rish care—
Hath bowed the spirit down in pain,
　　Nor set its signet there—
But like the flowers that bloom in Spring,
　　Or like the angels bright,
It scatters round a joyousness,
　　A beauty and a light.

A bright connecting link it is
　　Of more than human birth,
'Twixt scenes of God's own Paradise
　　And dwellers on this earth.
Oh, would that we could bear for aye
　　The feelings of a child—
How sweet would be our path through life,
　　Our death how calm and mild.

TO IONE.

BY LEWIS F. THOMAS.

Oh Ione! oh Ione! my heart's long lov'd *ideal*,
The cherish'd idol of my soul, all beautiful and real;
Oh, thou hast been through days of gloom and many months of care,
The theme of one enduring thought—my hope and my despair.
Though like a moth, I have been lur'd from genial air and skies,
To flit awhile beneath the light that shone from other eyes,
Yet hath their fire ne'er scathéd me, and thine have shed the ray,
The holy sunshine of the soul, that lit my being's day.

Fair Ione! fair Ione! I 've sought in learned lore
The works of high Philosophy, that sages taught of yore;
I 've read of deeds of daring, for lady-love and fame,
And mark'd the bright and lofty course that wins an honor'd name;
I 've drunk at the Pierian fount that gushes forth in song,
And heard the poet's lay of love, in music float along;
But lore of Sage, and deed of Fame, and lay of Poesy—
I 've left them all, to roam alone, sweet girl, and muse on thee.

Dear Ione! dear Ione! the smiling stars, they say,
Hold myriads of destinies, depending on each ray;
But thou, love, art the cynosure, within whose sphere, must be
The revelation of my life—my will—my destiny.
For oh, I feel that it is thine, and it is thine alone,
To mingle with my very mind, and make each thought thine own;
To bid me up the steep ascent, to grasp Ambition's crown,
Or bring me with my shatter'd hopes, all broken-hearted, down.

O Ione! O Ione! my heart may broken be,
But I'll not reck a broken heart, if broken 't is for thee.
And, oh! I would not, for the rule of monarch proud and high,
E'er cause a blush to light thy cheek, or tear to dim thine eye.
For me, then, suffer not regret to mar thy spirit's mirth,
And heed not, if my pathway be in dreariness and dearth;
And though the sky above *my* course, be dark and tempest-riven,
Be *thine* an ever-glorious day—an ever-smiling heaven.

LINES OF THE LIFE TO COME.

BY OTWAY CURRY.

> "Life, like a dome of many-colored glass,
> Stains the white radiance of eternity." SHELLEY.

Our spirit seeks a far-off clime
    All beautiful and pure,
Where living light, and sinless time,
    For evermore endure.

We spend our long and weary hours
    In dreaming of that shore,
Where all those perished hopes of ours
    Have swiftly gone before.

And do we yearn and strive in vain
    To rend the enshrouding pall,
That round us in this life of pain
    Lies like a dungeon wall?

Yes! for it clogs our halting thought,
    And dims our feeble light;—
How hardly is our spirit taught
    To shape its upward flight.

We strive with earthly imagings
    To reach and understand
The wondrous and the fearful things
    Of an Eternal Land.

We talk of amaranthine bowers
    And living groves of palm,
Of starry crowns, and fadeless flowers,
    And skies forever calm.

We talk of wings and raiment white,
    And pillared thrones of gold,
And cities built with jewels bright,
    Far in the Heavens, of old.

Are these things more than fancy's play?
    Are they, in very deed,
The free soul's guerdon far away,
    Its everlasting meed?

Or shall the spirit, in its flight
    Beyond the stars sublime,
See nothing but the radiance white
    Of never-ending time?

Shall things material change again,
    And wholly be forgot?
And round us only God remain,
    A universe of thought?

We know not well—we cannot know:
    Our reason's glimmering light
Can nothing but the darkness show
    Of our surrounding night.

But soon the doubt, and toil, and strife,
    Of earth shall all be done,
And knowledge of our endless life
    Be in a moment won.

TO A LADY,

WHO WONDERED WHY SHE WAS LOVED.

BY JAMES H. PERKINS.

It is not learning's borrowed gleam,
    It is not beauty's holier light,
It is not wealth, that makes thee seem
    So lovely in our sight.

The worth may leave Potosi's ore,
    Golconda's diamond lose its sheen,
But thine is the exhaustless store
    Of innocence serene.

The beauty of the eye must fade,
   The beauty of the cheek decay,
But from thy spirit, guileless maid,
   No charm shall pass away.

The learning of the gifted mind,
   Its gathered wisdom, may depart,
But in thy ignorance, I find
   The wisdom of the heart.

And that, nor earthly change nor ill,
   Nor time nor malady can blight;
And it is that, that makes thee still
   So lovely in our sight.

THE PIONEERS.

BY CHARLES A. JONES.

Where are the hardy yeomen
   Who battled for this land,
And trode these hoar old forests,
   A brave and gallant band?
Oh, know ye where they slumber
   No monument appears,

For Freedom's pilgrims to draw nigh,
    And hallow with their tears?
Or were no works of glory
    Done in the olden time?
And has the West no story
    Of deathless deeds sublime?

Go ask yon shining river,
    And it will tell a tale
Of deeds of noble daring,
    Will make thy cheek grow pale:
Go ask yon smiling valley,
    Whose harvest blooms so fair,
'T will tell thee a sad story
    Of the brave who slumber there:
Go ask yon mountain, rearing
    Its forest crest so high;
Each tree upon its summit,
    Has seen a warrior die.

They knew no dread of danger,
    When rose the Indian's yell;
Right gallantly they struggled,
    Right gallantly they fell:
From Alleghany's summit,
    To the farthest western shore,
These brave men's bones are lying
    Where they perished in their gore;

And not a single monument
  Is seen in all the land,
In honor of the memory
  Of that heroic band.

Their bones were left to whiten
  The spot where they were slain;
And were ye now to seek them,
  They would be sought in vain.
The mountain cat has feasted
  Upon them as they lay;
Long, long ago they mingled,
  Again with other clay:
Their very names are dying,
  Unconsecrate by fame,
In oblivion they slumber,
  Our glory and our shame.

NEW-ENGLAND.

WRITTEN FOR A CELEBRATION, IN KENTUCKY, OF THE LANDING OF THE PILGRIMS AT PLYMOUTH.

BY GEORGE D. PRENTICE.

CLIME of the brave! the high heart's home!
   Laved by the wild and stormy sea!
Thy children, in this far-off land,
   Devote, to-day, their hearts to thee:
Our thoughts, despite of space and time,
To-day, are in our native clime,
Where passed our sinless years, and where
Our infant heads first bowed in prayer.

Stern land! we love thy woods and rocks,
   Thy rushing streams, thy winter glooms,
And memory, like a pilgrim gray,
   Kneels at thy temples and thy tombs:
The thoughts of these, where'er we dwell,
Come o'er us like a holy spell,
A star to light our path of tears,
A rainbow on the sky of years!

Above thy cold and rocky breast
   The tempest sweeps, the night-wind wails,

But virtue, peace, and love, like birds,
   Are nestled 'mid thy hills and vales;
And Glory o'er each plain and glen
Walks with thy free and iron men,
And lights her sacred beacon still
On Bennington and Bunker Hill.

TO ONE IN HEAVEN.

BY OTWAY CURRY.

> "The all of thee that cannot die
> Through dark and dread eternity,
>   Returns again to me;
> And more thy buried love endears
> Than aught except its living years."   BYRON.

I know thou art gone to a clime of light
   All starry and gem-besprent—
Beyond the reach of the sunbeam's flight,
   In the far-off firmament.

The spirit, they say, cannot feel regret
   In that strange shining world of bliss,
But, free from pain, will forever forget
   The children of sorrow in this.

Oh! think not my heart one moment could deem
   So lightly of feelings like thine;
Though distant to them thy spirit may seem,
   I know thou art present with mine.

Thou art here again, where oft thou hast stood
   To list to the lulling chime
Of the wandering breeze in the waving wood,
   And the songs of the olden time.

Thou art watching the falling leaves that wake
   The waves in the tranquil stream,
Serene as the slumber that never can break,
   Or the joy of an endless dream.

And I will rejoice in thy presence again,
   And haply thy whisper shall hear,
Dispelling the gloom of sorrow and pain,
   When the twilight of death is near.

TO AN INDIAN MOUND.

BY THOMAS H. SHREVE.

Whence, and why art thou here, mysterious mound?
   Are questions which man asks, but asks in vain;
For o'er thy destinies a night profound,
   All rayless and all echoless, doth reign.
A thousand years have passed like yesterday,
   Since wint'ry snows first on thy bosom slept,
And much of mortal grandeur passed away,
   Since thou hast here thy voiceless vigils kept.

While standing thus upon thy oak-crowned head,
   The shadows of dim ages long since gone
Reel on my mind, like spectres of the dead,
   While dirge-like music haunts the wind's low moan.
From out the bosom of the boundless Past
   There rises up no voice of thee to tell:
Eternal silence, like a shadow vast,
   Broods on thy breast, and shrouds thine annals well.

Didst thou not antedate the rise of Rome,
   Egyptia's pyramids, and Grecian arts?
Did not the wild deer here for shelter come
   Before the Tyrrhene sea had ships or marts?
Through shadows deep and dark the mind must pierce,
   Which glances backward to that ancient time:

Nations before it fall in struggles fierce,
    Where human glory fades in human crime.

Upon the world's wide stage full many a scene
    Of grandeur and of gloom, of blood and blight,
Hath been enacted since thy forests green
    Sighed in the breeze and smiled in morning's light.
Thou didst not hear the woe, nor heed the crime,
    Which darken'd earth through ages of distress;
Unknowing and unknown, thou stood'st sublime,
    And calmly looked upon the wilderness.

The red man oft hath lain his aching head,
    When weary of the chase, upon thy breast;
And as the slumberous hours fast o'er him fled,
    Has dreamed of hunting-grounds in climes most blest.
Perhaps his thoughts ranged through the long past time,
    Striving to solve the problem of thy birth,
Till wearied out with dreams, dim though sublime,
    His fancy fluttered back to him and earth.

The eagle soaring through the upper air,
    Checks his proud flight, and glances on thy crest,
As though his destiny were pictured there,
    In the deep solitude that wraps thy breast.
Thy reign must soon be o'er—the human tide
    Is surging round thee like a restless sea;
And thou must yield thy empire and thy pride,
    And, like thy builders, soon forgotten be.

WAR SONG OF SEVENTY-SIX.

BY FREDERIC W. THOMAS.

Freemen! arise, and keep your vow!
    The foe are on our shore,
And we must win our freedom now,
    Or yield forevermore.

The share will make a goodly glave—
    Then tear it from the plough!
Lingers there here a crouching slave?
    Depart, a recreant thou!

Depart, and leave the field to those
    Determined to be free,
Who burn to meet their vaunting foes
    And strike for liberty.

Why did the pilgrim cross the wave?
    Say, was he not your sire?
And shall the liberty he gave
    Upon his grave expire?

The stormy wave could not appal;
    Nor where the savage trod;

He braved them all, and conquered all,
    For freedom and for God.

We fight for fireside and for home,
    For heritage, for altar;
And by the God of yon blue dome,
    Not one of us shall falter!

We 'll guard them though the foeman stood
    Like sand-grains on our shore,
And raise our angry battle flood
    And whelm the despots o'er.

We 've drawn the sword, and shrined the sheath
    Upon our fathers' tomb;
And when the foe shall sleep in death,
    We 'll sheath it o'er their doom.

Firm be your step, steady your file,
    Unbroken your array:
The spirits of the blest shall smile,
    Upon our deeds to-day.

Unfurl the banner of the free
    Amidst the battle's cloud;
Its folds shall wave to Liberty
    Or be to us a shroud.

O'er those who fall, the soldier's tear
    Exulting shall be shed;

We 'll bear them upon honor's bier,
    To sleep in honor's bed.

The maiden with her hurried breath
    And rapture-beaming eye,
Shall all forget the field of death
    To bless the victory.

The child, oh! he will bless his sire,
    The mother bless her son,
And God, He will not frown in ire,
    When such a field is won.

THE BACKWOODSMAN.

BY EPHRAIM PEABODY.

The silent wilderness for me!
    Where never sound is heard,
Save the rustling of the squirrel's foot,
    And the flitting wing of bird,
Or its low and interrupted note,
    And the deer's quick, crackling tread,
And the swaying of the forest boughs,
    As the wind moves overhead.

Alone, (how glorious to be free!)
   My good dog at my side,
My rifle hanging in my arm,
   I range the forests wide.
And now the regal buffalo
   Across the plains I chase;
Now track the mountain stream, to find
   The beaver's lurking place.

I stand upon the mountain's top,
   And (solitude profound!)
Not even a woodman's smoke curls up
   Within the horizon's bound.
Below, as o'er its ocean breadth
   The air's light currents run,
The wilderness of moving leaves
   Is glancing in the sun.

I look around to where the sky
   Meets the far forest line,
And this imperial domain—
   This kingdom—all is mine.
This bending heaven—these floating clouds—
   Waters that ever roll—
And wilderness of glory, bring
   Their offerings to my soul.

My palace, built by God's own hand,
   The world's fresh prime hath seen;

Wide stretch its living halls away,
  Pillared and roofed with green.
My music is the wind that now
  Pours loud its swelling bars,
Now lulls in dying cadences,—
  My festal lamps are stars.

Though when, in this my lonely home,
  My star-watched couch I press,
I hear no fond " good night"—think not
  I am companionless.
O no! I see my father's house,
  The hill, the tree, the stream,
And the looks and voices of my home
  Come gently to my dream.

And in these solitary haunts,
  While slumbers every tree
In night and silence, God himself
  Seems nearer unto me.
I *feel* His presence in these shades
  Like the embracing air;
And as my eye-lids close in sleep,
  My heart is hushed in prayer.

OF ONE NOW FAR AWAY.

BY JAMES H. PERKINS.

Late to our town there came a maid,
   A noble woman, true and pure;
Who, in the little while she staid,
   Wrought works that will endure.

It was not any thing she said;
   It was not any thing she did:—
It was the movement of her head,—
   The lifting of her lid;

Her little motions when she spoke,—
   The presence of an upright soul,—
The living light that from her broke,—
   It was the perfect whole:

We saw it in her floating hair,
   We saw it in her laughing eye;—
For every look and feature there,
   Wrought works that cannot die.

For she to many among us gave
   A reverence for the true, the pure,
The perfect,—that has power to save,
   And make the doubting, sure.

She passed ; she went to other lands ;
    She knew not of the work she did :
The wondrous product of her hands
    From her is ever hid.

Forever, did I say ? Oh no !
    The time must come when she will look
Upon her pilgrimage below,
    And find it in God's Book,

That as she trod her path aright,
    Power from her very garments stole ;—
For such is the mysterious might
    God grants the upright soul.

A deed, a word, our careless rest,
    A simple thought, a common feeling,—
If He be present in the breast,
    Has from Him powers of healing.

Go, maiden ; with thy golden tresses,
    Thine azure eye, and changing cheek,—
Go, and forget the one who blesses
    Thy presence through that week.

Forget him : he will not forget ;
    But strive to live, and testify
Thy goodness,—when Earth's sun has set,
    And Time itself rolled by.

MY NATIVE LAND.

BY HUGH PETERS.

'My Native Land, good night.' —BYRON.

THE boat swings from the pebbled shore,
    And proudly drives her prow;
The crested waves roll up before:—
Yon dark gray land, I see no more,
    How sweet it seemeth now!
Thou dark gray land, my native land,
    Thou land of rock and pine,
I 'm speeding from thy golden sand;
But can I wave a farewell hand
    To such a shore as thine?

I 've gazed upon the golden cloud
    Which shades thine emerald sod;
Thy hills, which Freedom's share hath plough'd,
Which nurse a race that have not bow'd
    Their knee to aught but God;
Thy mountain floods which proudly fling
    Their waters to the fall—
Thy birds, which cut with rushing wing
The sky that greets thy coming spring,
    And thought thy glories small.

But now ye 've shrunk to yon blue line
   Between the sky and sea,
I feel, sweet home, that thou art mine,
I feel my bosom cling to thine—
   That I am part of thee.
I see thee blended with the wave,
   As children see the earth
Close up a sainted mother's grave;
They weep for her they cannot save,
   And feel her holy worth.

Thou mountain land—thou land of rock,
   I 'm proud to call thee free;
Thy sons are of the pilgrim stock,
And nerved like those who stood the shock
   At old Thermopylæ.
The laurel wreaths their fathers won,
   The children wear them still—
Proud deeds those iron men have done,
They fought and won at Bennington,
   And bled at Bunker Hill.

There 's grandeur in the lightning stroke
   That rives thy mountain ash;
There 's glory in thy giant oak,
And rainbow beauty in the smoke
   Where crystal waters dash:
There 's music in thy winter blast
   That sweeps the hollow glen;

Less sturdy sons would shrink aghast
From piercing winds like those thou hast
   To nurse thine iron men.

And thou hast gems; ay, living pearls;
   And flowers of Eden hue:
Thy loveliest, are thy bright-eyed girls,
Of fairy forms and elfin curls,
   And smiles like Hermon's dew:
They 've hearts like those they 're born to wed,
   Too proud to nurse a slave;
They 'd scorn to share a monarch's bed,
And sooner lay their angel head
   Deep in their humble grave.

And I have left thee, Home, alone,
   A pilgrim from thy shore;
The wind goes by with hollow moan,
I hear it sigh a warning tone,
   "Ye see your home no more."
I 'm cast upon the world's wide sea,
   Torn like an ocean weed;
I 'm cast away, far, far from thee,
I feel a thing I cannot be,
   A bruised and broken reed.

Farewell, my native land, farewell!
   That wave has hid thee now—

My heart is bow'd as with a spell.
This rending pang!—would I could tell
   What ails my throbbing brow!
One look upon that fading streak
   Which bounds yon eastern sky;
One tear to cool my burning cheek;
And then a word I cannot speak—
   "My native land—Good bye."

LINES,

WITH A SKETCH OF JACOB'S WELL, AND MOUNT GERIZIM.

BY JAMES F. CLARKE.

Here, after Jacob parted from his brother,
   His daughters lingered round this well, new made;
Here—seventeen centuries after, came another
   And talked with Jesus, wondering and afraid.
Here—other centuries past—the emperor's mother,
   Sheltered its waters with a Temple's shade.
Here—'mid the fallen fragments, as of old,
The girl her pitcher dips within its waters cold.

And Jacob's race grew strong for many an hour,
   Then torn beneath the Roman eagle lay;

The Roman's vast and earth-controlling power,
    Has crumbled like these shafts and stones away:
But still the waters, fed by dew and shower,
    Come up, as ever, to the light of day—
And still the maid bends downward with her urn,
Well pleased to see its glass her lovely face return.

And those few words of truth, first uttered here,
    Have sunk into the human soul and heart;
A spiritual faith dawns bright and clear,
    Dark creeds and ancient mysteries depart;
The hour for God's true worshippers draws near;
    Then mourn not o'er the wrecks of earthly art—
Kingdoms may fall, and human works decay,
Nature moves on unchanged—*Truths* never pass away.

HAPPINESS: A PICTURE.

BY WILLIAM D. GALLAGHER.

A GREEN lawn, and a humble cot
    Embowered in vines and spreading trees;
Before the door a verdant plot,
    And flowers whose perfume loads the breeze:
Upon the grass, those flowers among,
    Glad as the winds that thither stray,

A group of children, fair and young,—
  Their cheeks are flush'd with play!

Midway the two small rooms between,
  (For only two hath cot like this,)
Spectator of the joyous scene,
  And sharer of the heart-felt bliss,
A white-haired grandam;—on her knee
  Her knitting lies neglected now;
She fairly strains her eyes to see,—
  Her specs pushed to her brow!

A smile illumes her withered cheeks,—
  On each a glistening tear-drop lies;
Her lips apart—she thoughtless speaks,
  And harder strains her filmy eyes.
One now its playful fellows leaves,
  And toward her springs with all its might;
Her heart is full—her bosom heaves
  With love's intense delight.

An instant, and it dropt to earth,
  As if a death-stroke laid it low:
A chill ran through her frame—her mirth
  Was changed as instantly to wo.
It shriek'd aloud!—she forward sprung,
  And caught it to her panting breast:
A bee its tiny foot had stung,
  On clover blossom press'd.

THE FLIGHT OF YEARS.

BY GEORGE D. PRENTICE.

GONE! gone forever!—Like a rushing wave
Another year has burst upon the shore
Of earthly being—and its last low tones,
Wandering in broken accents on the air,
Are dying to an echo.

            The gay Spring,
With its young charms, has gone—gone with its leaves—
Its atmosphere of roses—its white clouds
Slumbering like seraphs in the air—its birds
Telling their loves in music—and its streams
Leaping and shouting from the up-piled rocks
To make earth echo with the joy of waves.
And Summer, with its dews and showers, has gone—
Its rainbows glowing on the distant cloud
Like Spirits of the Storm—its peaceful lakes
Smiling in their sweet sleep, as if their dreams
Were of the opening flowers and budding trees
And overhanging sky—and its bright mists
Resting upon the mountain-tops, as crowns
Upon the heads of giants. Autumn too
Has gone, with all its deeper glories—gone
With its green hills like altars of the world

Lifting their rich fruit-offerings to their God—
Its cool winds straying 'mid the forest aisles
To wake their thousand wind-harps—its serene
And holy sunsets hanging o'er the West
Like banners from the battlements of Heaven—
And its still evenings, when the moonlit sea
Was ever throbbing, like the living heart
Of the great Universe. Ay—these are now
But sounds and visions of the past—their deep,
Wild beauty has departed from the Earth,
And they are gathered to the embrace of Death,
Their solemn herald to Eternity.

Nor have they gone alone. High human hearts
Of Passion have gone with them. The fresh dust
Is chill on many a breast, that burned erewhile
With fires that seemed immortal. Joys, that leaped
Like angels from the heart, and wandered free
In life's young morn to look upon the flowers
The poetry of nature, and to list
The woven sounds of breeze, and bird, and stream,
Upon the night-air, have been stricken down
In silence to the dust. Exultant Hope,
That roved forever on the buoyant winds
Like the bright, starry bird of Paradise,
And chaunted to the ever-listening heart
In the wild music of a thousand tongues,
Or soared into the open sky, until
Night's burning gems seemed jewelled on her brow,

Has shut her drooping wing, and made her home
Within the voiceless sepulchre. And Love,
That knelt at Passion's holiest shrine, and gazed
On his heart's idol as on some sweet star,
Whose purity and distance make it dear,
And dreamed of ecstacies, until his soul
Seemed but a lyre, that wakened in the glance
Of the beloved one—he too has gone
To his eternal resting place. And where
Is stern Ambition—he who madly grasped
At Glory's fleeting phantom—he who sought
His fame upon the battle-field, and longed
To make his throne a pyramid of bones
Amid a sea of blood? He too has gone!
His stormy voice is mute—his mighty arm
Is nerveless on its clod—his very name
Is but a meteor of the night of years
Whose gleams flashed out a moment o'er the Earth,
And faded into nothingness. The dream
Of high devotion—beauty's bright array—
And life's deep idol memories—all have passed
Like the cloud-shadows on a starlight stream,
Or a soft strain of music, when the winds
Are slumbering on the billow.

     Yet, why muse
Upon the past with sorrow? Though the year
Has gone to blend with the mysterious tide
Of old Eternity, and borne along

Upon its heaving breast a thousand wrecks
Of glory and of beauty—yet, why mourn
That such is destiny? Another year
Succeedeth to the past—in their bright round
The seasons come and go—the same blue arch,
That hath hung o'er us, will hang o'er us yet—
The same pure stars that we have lov'd to watch,
Will blossom still at twilight's gentle hour
Like lilies on the tomb of Day—and still
Man will remain, to dream as he hath dreamed,
And mark the earth with passion. Love will spring
From the lone tomb of old Affections—Hope
And Joy and great Ambition, will rise up
As they have risen—and their deeds will be
Brighter than those engraven on the scroll
Of parted centuries. Even now the sea
Of coming years, beneath whose mighty waves
Life's great events are heaving into birth,
Is tossing to and fro, as if the winds
Of heaven were prisoned in its soundless depths
And struggling to be free.

                    Weep not, that Time
Is passing on—it will ere long reveal
A brighter era to the nations. Hark!
Along the vales and mountains of the earth
There is a deep, portentous murmuring,
Like the swift rush of subterranean streams,
Or like the mingled sounds of earth and air,

When the fierce Tempest, with sonorous wing,
Heaves his deep folds upon the rushing winds,
And hurries onward with his night of clouds
Against the eternal mountains.   'T is the voice
Of infant FREEDOM—and her stirring call
Is heard and answered in a thousand tones
From every hill-top of her western home—
And lo—it breaks across old Ocean's flood—
And " FREEDOM! FREEDOM!" is the answering shout
Of nations starting from the spell of years.
The day-spring!—see—'t is brightening in the heavens!
The watchmen of the night have caught the sign—
From tower to tower the signal-fires flash free—
And the deep watch-word, like the rush of seas
That heralds the volcano's bursting flame,
Is sounding o'er the earth.   Bright years of hope
And life are on the wing!—Yon glorious bow
Of Freedom, bended by the hand of God,
Is spanning Time's dark surges.   Its high Arch,
A type of Love and Mercy on the cloud,
Tells, that the many storms of human life
Will pass in silence, and the sinking waves,
Gathering the forms of glory and of peace,
Reflect the undimmed brightness of the Heavens.

TO THE STAR LYRA.

BY WILLIAM WALLACE.

Harp of Eternity!—thy strings
   Ten thousand thousand years have told,
Since o'er thy frame the mystic wings
   Of time unwearied roll'd;
And still from that mysterious throne
Thy song, magnificent and lone,
   Peals nightly as of old,
When Chaldea's Shepherd bent his ear
To catch the music of each sphere.

How fondly gazed that old man round
   The dread magnificence above,
Woo'd by the anthem's mellow sound,
   Breathing of seraph love;
Whose brooding wings shed deathless bliss
O'er pensile orb and starr'd abyss,
   Like Heaven's own holy dove—
For he, on those high rocks, had caught
Beams from the Spirit-land of thought;

And heard thy music, mighty Lyre,
   Struck by the giant hand of Time,
Rolling amid yon worlds of fire,
   Their choral march sublime.

How leap'd his heart—how swell'd his soul—
To hear those awful numbers roll
   In one eternal chime ;
And dream that, freed from Earth's dark sod,
Already he communed with God!

Bard of the stars! Thou led'st the dance
   Of thrice ten thousand thousand spheres,
Wheeling in their delirious trance
   'Through the unnumbered years.
Unmoved alike 'mid life or death—
The storm's career—the tempest's breath,
   Or folly—crime and tears—
Still! still behind those cloudy bars,
Glitters the Poet of the Stars!

Thou art alone!—At twilight dim,
   And in the Night's transparent noon,
Solemnly weaving thy wild hymn,
   And solitary tune,
Like some sad Hermit,—whose lone heart
Would from all earthly splendors part,
   Lured by their glare too soon,
And 'mid the Desert's silent gloom
Wait uncomplainingly its doom.

Alone! oh, sacred ONE,—dost thou
   From that star-cinctur'd hall, behold
Sorrows which scathe the human brow,
   And griefs that burn untold,

Save to the night-winds drooping by—
Like mourners journeying from the sky—
   Coldly and dark unroll'd?
Vainly we ask, or low, or loud,
Bright Minstrel of the star and cloud.

Sound on, oh mighty Harp! Thy strain
   Comes floating sadly on the night—
For we may ne'er behold again
   Thy pure and sacred light,
But in the cold insensate tomb,
Rest all unknowingly our doom;
   While thou, intensely bright,
Shalt pour thy glorious music still,
Alike unscath'd by death or ill.

Sound on! But those sweet harps of earth,
   Whose strings lie shattered, cold and lone,
Shall yet, restored by godlike worth,
   Resume their godlike tone;
While thou must be, oh! ancient lyre,
Destroyed in Nature's funeral pyre,
   And broken on thy throne—
Where they—undimm'd by earth-born jars—
May lead, like thee, the dance of stars!

Oh, glorious hope! Oh, thought divine!
   Soul! fired by the high-promised bliss,

Kneel at thy God's eternal shrine,
  And breathe thy thanks for this!
Harp! lift once more thy joyous song—
Bear its—oh, bear its notes along,
  O'er earth and far abyss!
Hail with a smile Death's gloomy frown,—
Spirit! he brings thy brightest crown!

HYMN.

BY JAMES H. PERKINS.

By earth hemmed in, by earth oppressed,
  'T is hard to labor; hard to pray:
And of the week, for prayer and rest
  We 've but one Sabbath day.

But purer spirits walk above,
  Who worship alway; who are blest
With an upspringing might of love,
  That makes all labor rest.

Father! while here, I would arise
  In spirit to that realm; and there,
Be every act a sacrifice,
  And every thought a prayer.

TRUTH AND MISANTHROPY.

BY JACOB W. ELY.

Oh his heart was sad in his early day,
    When the lights of youth around him shone,
And beamed from the brows of the young and gay,
    As tireless time danced gayly on—
But in friendship's throng, when the soul rose high,
And pleasure shone from the sparkling eye,
And the heart breathed forth a warmth and truth,
Which it only feels in the days of youth,
A voice to his heart would coldly say,
'What dost thou here? away! away!'

Hope led him on, to the fountain bright,
    That flows around love's flowery fane,
Where the heart which once has drunk delight,
    Can never taste its sweets again.
And he long'd to love, but a voice would say,
'No heart is thine—away! away!'—
And dark was the cloud, that rose to press
On his soul in its utter loneliness;
And a withered heart, and a burning brain,
Might tell he had deeply loved in vain.

He flew to the bowl, the Lethean spring,
    Where weary and joyless spirits quaffed;
And his shout rose high in the reeling ring,
    As he deeply drank and madly laughed:
But a voice soon thundered on his soul,
' Away, away from the mad'ning bowl—
The light that glances round its brim,
As ye deeply drink, will grow more dim,
And the sparkling draught ye love so well
Will sear the heart, like the blasts of hell'!'

The wanderer woke from a sleepless dream,
    That had bound his soul for many a day,
And friendship's name, and love's soft gleam,
    And the mad'ning bowl, had passed away—
And the voice of *Truth*, his guardian, spoke:
' Look forth on the world, the spell is broke—
Look forth, look forth, and thou may'st see
The world in its base deformity—
Though many lights are gleaming there,
Thou know'st how *deeply false they are.*'

WESTERN SCENERY.

BY EPHRAIM PEABODY.

Morn on the Alleghanies! on their side,
Crossing a rocky promontory's brow,
That juts out o'er the wilderness below,
A band of emigrants may be descried.
Dawn on the mountains! Gloriously the morn
Purples along the east. The stars are shorn
And struggle forward with thin rays and white,
Then fade and vanish in the advancing light.
O'er the far forest-line, the herald-beams
Of morning upward blaze in rushing streams;
And the imperial sun, as he ascends,
 His sceptred rays extends
To the far summits that to heaven aspire—
And at the touch they glow with heaven's own fire.
 The awaking mountain-breezes lift
The mists that hang in the deep vales, and drift
Their folds, now fiery, and now dark, aloft—
 They rise—scattered, and thin, and soft—
The incense of these mountain altars—to the clear,
 Blue dome of heaven, and disappear.
As touched by Prospero's wand, a wide expanse
Opens at once upon their backward glance;

Far down—a circling vale, wherein the might
Of nations could do battle for a nation's right;
Around—heights over heights the vale embrace,
Like levels round some vast arena's space;
And far beyond, the clouds around them furl'd,
Heaves each long mountain-range—a rampart of the world.

Upon the naked promontory's brow
That overhung the wilderness below,
The travellers paused to look upon the scene.
The wife upon her husband's arm did lean,
And he upon his rifle, silently.
Hushed even was happy childhood's morning glee.
The vastness of the scene weighed down the sense,
And man felt nothing but his impotence,
And His supremacy who reigns *alone*,
" The earth his footstool, and the heavens his throne."

Sublimest was the awful silence there,
Hushing the very progress of the air.
Through the deep vale below a river flowed,
Falling, at times, in silver sheets—then hid
   The o'erhanging wilderness amid—
Now hurrying 'tween the jagged rocks and rude;
Yet not a murmur rose to where they stood.
The infrequent clouds drifted athwart the sky,
Ever and ever floating silently.
Upon the topmost crag, splintered and bare,
Its angles glittering in the morning's glare,

  With an unsteady wing
  And naked talons, balancing,
 An eagle sat and screamed t' the silence;—hill,
And wood, and silent cloud, echoed his accents shrill.

THE TUMULUS.

WRITTEN UPON VISITING ONE OF THE STUPENDOUS MOUNDS THAT GREET THE EYE OF THE TRAVELLER IN THE WEST.

BY MRS. JULIA L. DUMONT.

ETERNAL vestige of departed years!
Mysterious signet of a race gone by,
Unscath'd while Ruin o'er the earth careers,
And round thy base the wrecks of ages lie.
Reveal'st thou nought to the inquiring eye?
What fearful changes Time has given birth
Since first thy form, where now the oak towers high,
A dark gray mass, rose from the verdant earth.

Ah! where are those who proudly trod thy brow,
Ere yet thy bright green coronals waved there—
The strong, the brave, their race—where is it now?
Earth's living nations no memorial bear!

Where then the sounds of life rose on the air,
A grave-like silence, long and deep, has pass'd,
Save when the wolf howl'd from his rocky lair,
Or owlet-screams rose on the fitful blast.

Bear'st thou no trace within thy sullen breast,
Thou seal'd-up relick of the mouldering dead?
Is there no record on thy form imprest
Of those who rear'd thee from thy valley bed?
Did pale Decay, with slow though lingering tread,
Consign their race to nature's common tomb?
Or sweeping Plague, with blasting wing outspread,
Their brightness quench in everlasting gloom?

And thou, that mock'st Destruction's wrathful storm,
While living worlds beneath its blast are crush'd,
Say for what end the dead upheav'd thy form,
Or consecrated thus thy breathless dust.
Did calm Devotion here, with holy trust,
Erect her temple to the living God?
Or lordly Pride, with weak ambition flush'd,
Heap up thy dark and monumental sod?

Or hid'st thou those, in thy sepulchral breast,
Who erst were scattered o'er the vales around?
A mighty tomb, where nations, laid to rest
In ghastly sleep, await the trumpet's sound.
When Earth's dim records are at length unbound,
And in her last funereal lights reveal'd,

While rising bones burst from their prison ground,
Shall then thy heaving brow its mysteries yield?

Vainly I ask—but o'er the musing soul
A noiseless voice comes from thy dust to chide:
"Man may exult in glory's glittering roll,
And o'er the earth, life, for a while preside;
But learn to know the wreck of human pride!
Her fairest names time may at length efface;
Dark o'er her cities flow Oblivion's tide,
And Death abide where life and joy have place."

THE BLISS OF HOME.

BY THOMAS H. SHREVE.

Mine be the joy which gleams around
    The hearth where pure affections dwell—
Where love enrobed in smiles is found,
    And wraps the spirit with its spell.

I would not seek excitement's whirl,
    Where Pleasure wears her tinsel crown,
And Passion's billows upward curl,
    'Neath Hatred's darkly gathering frown.

The dearest boon from heaven above,
   Is bliss which brightly hallows home—
The sunlight of our world of love,
   Unknown to those who reckless roam.

There is a sympathy of heart
   Which consecrates the social shrine,
Robs grief of gloom, and doth impart
   A joy to gladness all divine.

It glances from the kindling eye,
   Which o'er Affliction sleepless tends—
It gives deep pathos to the sigh
   Which anguish from the bosom rends.

It plays around the smiling lip,
   When Love bestows the greeting kiss—
And sparkles in each cup we sip
   Round the domestic board in bliss!

Let others seek in Wealth or Fame,
   A splendid path whereon to tread—
I'd rather wear a lowlier name,
   With Love's enchantments round it shed.

Fame's but a light to gild the grave,
   And Wealth can never calm the breast—
But Love, a halcyon on Life's wave,
   Hath power to soothe its strifes to rest.

CONNECTICUT: A FRAGMENT.

BY HUGH PETERS.

"Young thoughts have music in them."—HALLECK.

I LOVED to sit at night upon thy grass,
   CONNECTICUT, and hear the night air creep
Across the leaves ;—to see the white clouds pass
   Before the morn, and shroud the hills in deep,
Dark shade ; and then to hear some clear-voiced lass,
   In tones so soft and sad they made one weep,
From some still porch, breathe out a song to me,
Like this—a sweet but plaintive melody :

   " There 's music in the gush of streams
      When winter leaves the land :—
   There 's music in the April breeze,
      Which, beautiful and bland,
   Comes rushing from the far South-west
      Towards the burning zone :—
   They have such in CONNECTICUT,
    ' My beautiful, my own.'

   There 's music in the voice of birds,
      Hailing the coming morn ;—

There 's music in the bleat of lambs,
    And in the hunter's horn—
There 's music ' in the laugh of girls,'
    A thrill in every tone;
Such girls as thine, CONNECTICUT,
    ' My beautiful, my own.'

They say there 's music in the air,
    Up in the deep blue sky—
Where angels pour, from golden harps,
    Unearthly melody—
I used to think I heard it there
    When standing all alone,
At midnight, in CONNECTICUT,
    ' My beautiful, my own.'

The rushing wind which curls the sea,
    Has ' music in its roar:'
And so has that which whistles through
    The key-hole of my door:
And that which wreaths the hills with snow,
    Has music in its moan—
Those hills of thine, CONNECTICUT,
    ' My beutiful, my own.'

There 's music in the deep low tones
    Of holy men at prayer,—
Which steals us from our worldliness,
    Our miseries, our care:

Such prayers as oft are heard around
　The hearth's pure altar stone,
On Sundays, in CONNECTICUT,
　'My beautiful, my own.'

There's music in the bosom of
　The home-bound wanderer,
When first his eager glances spy
　His boyhood's haunts, afar:
I hear such music, when in dreams
　All wearied, and alone,
I visit thee, CONNECTICUT,
　'My beautiful, my own.'

There's music, ay, in every thing,
　On earth, in sea, or air:
The ocean's murmurings are hymns,
　The wind's low whispers, prayer—
And these from shore and hill I've heard
　Go up to God's high throne,
In thy fair land, CONNECTICUT,
　'My beautiful, my own.'

EPILOGUE.

SPOKEN BY A THESPIAN AT AN ENTERTAINMENT IN CIN-
CINNATI FOR THE BENEFIT OF THE POOR.

BY MRS. CAROLINE LEE HENTZ.

We 've met in Fancy's dedicated hall,
But not *alone* at Pleasure's siren call:
Here, in this temple, where the tragic Muse,
Her dark locks heavy with Olympian dews,
So oft in all the pomp of vision'd wo,
Has bid the holy drops of pity flow,
We 've gather'd—by a nobler purpose led,—
To dry the tear by *real* misery shed.

An angel spirit o'er the scene presides,
And round these walls with sheltering pinions glides,
Oh, Charity! thou Hierarch of heaven,
To *thee,* this night, our offerings be given,—
Accept the fragrant incense of the heart—
The flowers of nature, and the gems of art.
Has music charm'd us with her tuneful tongue?
Thy seraph strains with *hers* responsive rung.
Has eloquence enchain'd the captive soul?
Thy inspiration bade the numbers roll.

Sweet is the melody of choral song,
When beauty's lips the dulcet notes prolong;
But sweeter still, the helpless orphan's prayer,
The lonely widow's, who our bounty share.
Rich are the tones of rhetoric, but still
More rich, ennobling, are the sounds which thrill
In Pity's ear, when grateful Want receives
The boon, which Penury's keen pang relieves.

Hark! on the stillness of the wintry night,
What wild alarum breaks? What flashing light
Streams, like war's banner through the midnight gloom?
Ah! many a trembling victim reads its doom
In that destroying element's red glare,
Written in lines of desolation there.
Where shall the houseless, homeless wanderers wend?
Heaven's cold, unsheltering arches o'er them bend.
Unpillowed misery weeps. Oh thou! whose power
Has wing'd and sanctified this festive hour,
Celestial Charity! these woes arrest;
Clasp the pale mourners to thy pitying breast;
Bind up each wound by human suffering made,
And gild, with cheering beam, afflictions darkest shade.

ON THE DEATH OF A YOUNG CHILD.

BY JAMES H. PERKINS.

STAND back; uncovered stand: for, lo!
The parents that have lost their child.
  Bow to the majesty of wo!

He came, an herald from above;
  Pure from his God he came to them,
Teaching new duties, deeper love;
  And, like the boy of Bethlehem,
He grew in stature, and in grace.
From the sweet spirit of his face
They learnt a new, more heavenly joy—
And were the better for their boy.

But God hath taken whom He gave;
  Recalled the Messenger He sent;
And now beside the infant's grave
  The spirit of the strong is bent.

But though the tears must flow; the heart
  Ache with its vacant, strange distress,
Ye did not from your infant part
  When his clear eye grew meaningless.
That eye is beaming still; and still
  Upon his Father's errand, he—

Your own dear, bright, unearthly boy—
   Worketh the kind, mysterious Will;
And from this fount of bitter grief
   Will bring a stream of joy.
Oh! may this be your faith, and your relief!

Then will the world be full of him; the sky,
With all its placid myriads, to your eye
Will tell of him; the wind will breathe his tone;
And slumbering in the midnight, they alone,
Your Father and your child, will hover nigh.
Believe in him, behold him everywhere,
And sin will die within you; earthly care
Fall to its earth—and Heavenward, side by side,
Ye shall go up, your infant for your guide.
Ye shall go up, beyond this realm of storms,
Quick, and more quick; till welcomed there above,
His voice shall bid ye, in the might of love,
Lay down these weeds of earth, and wear your native forms.

TO A BUNCH OF FLOWERS.

BY JAMES F. CLARKE.

LITTLE firstlings of the year!
Have you come my room to cheer?
You are dry and parched, I think,
Stand within this glass and drink;
Stand beside me on the table
'Mong my books—if I am able
I will find a vacant space
For your bashfulness and grace:
Learned tasks and serious duty
Shall be lightened by your beauty.

Pure affection's sweetest token,
Choicest hint of love unspoken,
Friendship in your help rejoices,
Uttering her mysterious voices.
You are gifts the poor may offer,—
Wealth can find no better proffer;
For you tell of tastes refined,
Thoughtful heart and spirit kind.
Gift of gold or jewel dresses
Ostentatious thought confesses;
Simplest mind this boon may give,
Modesty herself receive.

For lovely woman you were meant
The just and natural ornament,
Sleeping on her bosom fair,
Hiding in her raven hair;
Or peeping out 'mid golden curls,
You outshine barbaric pearls,
Yet you lead no thought astray,
Feed not pride nor vain display,
Nor disturb her sisters' rest,
Waking envy in their breast.

Let the rich, with heart elate,
Pile their board with costly plate,
Richer ornaments are ours,
We will dress our homes with flowers;
Yet no terror need we feel
Lest the thief break through to steal.

Ye are playthings for the child,
Gifts of love for maiden mild;
Comfort for the aged eye,
For the poor, cheap luxury.

Though your life is but a day,
Precious things, dear flowers, you say,
Telling that the Being good
Who supplies our daily food,
Deems it needful to supply
Daily food for heart and eye.

So, though your life is but a day,
We grieve not at your swift decay.
He, who smiles in your bright faces,
Sends us more to take your places.
'T is for this ye fade so soon,
That He may renew the boon:
That kindness often may repeat
These mute messages so sweet:
That Love to plainer speech may get,
Conning oft his alphabet:
That Beauty may be rained from heaven,
New with every morn and even,
With freshest fragrance sunrise greeting:
Therefore are ye, flowers, so fleeting.

ODE TO THE PRESS.

BY G. G. FOSTER.

As breaks the sun o'er ocean's gloom,
   And lights the dark and frowning sea—
While the frail bark, escaped its doom,
   Again sails onward fast and free—
So the dark world beneath thy light
Sprung up in intellectual might.

The pride, the pomp, the power of kings,
   Faded like mist before thy ray;
And men perceived these mighty things
   Dwindle to atoms, even as they—
While o'er the earth a SPIRIT went,
With voice and eye all eloquent.

The nations heard its voice, and all
   The populous millions of earth's slaves
Re-echoed with glad shout the call
   Of FREEDOM, standing o'er the graves
Of uncrowned kings, unmitred popes,
And all that crushed man's highest hopes.

No more the emancipated world
   Bowed 'neath the despot's iron rod;
The tyrant from his throne was hurl'd—
   Man, slave no more, assumed the god—
And Genius, with her arts sublime,
Gilded the wings of passing Time.

THE PARTING.

BY HUGH PETERS.

Their bark is out upon the sea,
   She leaps across the tide :—
The flashing waves dash joyously
   Their spray upon her side :
As if a bird, before the breeze
   She spreads her snowy wings,
And breaking through the crested seas,
   How beautiful she springs.

The deep blue sky above her path
   Is cloudless, and the air
That pure and spicy fragrance hath
   Which Ceylon's breezes bear—
And though she seems a shadowless
   And phantom thing, in sport,
Her freight I ween is Happiness,
   And Heaven her far-off port.

Mild, tearful eyes are gazing now
   Upon that fleeting ship,
And here, perhaps, an ashy brow,
   And there a trembling lip,

Are tokens of the agony,
    The pangs it costs to sever
A mother from her first born child,
    To say—farewell, forever.

And they who sail yon fading bark
    Have turned a yearning eye
To the far land which seems a line
    Between the sea and sky.
And as that land blends with the sea,
    Like clouds in sunset light,
A soft, low voice breathes on the wind,
    " My native land, good night."

And they who stand upon the shore,
    And bend them o'er the sea,
To catch the last, faint shadow of
    The shrouds' dim tracery,—
I ween if one could hear the sigh,
    Could catch the mother's tone,
He 'd hear it say, " Good night—good night,
    " My beautiful—my own."

That ship is gone, lost to the eye;
    But still a freshening breeze
Is o'er her wake, and drives her on
    Through smooth and pleasant seas.

Right onward thus, she will dash on,
　　　　Though tempests shake the air,
　　　For hearts that fear not ocean's wrath
　　　　I ween will aye be there.

　　　　　　*　　*　　*　　*

　　　That sea is Life.—That bark is but
　　　　The Hopes of wedded Love:
　　　The wind which fills its swelling sails
　　　　I trust is from above.
　　　And ever may its progress be
　　　　Through summer seas right on,
　　　Till blended with Eternity's
　　　　Broad ocean's horizon.

TO A MIDNIGHT PHANTOM.

BY OTWAY CURRY.

　　　PALE, melancholy one!
　　　　Why art thou lingering here?
　　　Memorial of dark ages gone,
　　　　Herald of darkness near:
　　　Thou stand'st immortal, undefiled—
　　　Even thou, the unknown, the strange, the wild,
　　　　Spell-word of mortal fear.

Thou art a shadowy form,
　　A dreamlike thing of air;
My very sighs thy robes deform,
　　So frail, so passing fair—
Thy crown is of the fabled gems,
The bright ephemeral diadems
　　That unseen spirits wear.

Thou hast revealed to me
　　The lore of phantom song,
With thy wild, fearful melody,
　　Chiming the whole night long
Forebodings of untimely doom,
Of sorrowing years and dying gloom,
　　And unrequited wrong.

Through all the dreary night,
　　Thine icy hands, that now
Send to the brain their maddening blight,
　　Have pressed upon my brow—
My phrenzied thoughts all wildly blend
With spell-wrought shapes that round me wend,
　　Or down in mockery bow.

Away, pale form, away—
　　The break of morn is nigh,
And far and dim, beyond the day
　　The eternal night-glooms lie:

Art thou a dweller in the dread
Assembly of the mouldering dead,
   Or in the worlds on high?

Art thou of the blue waves,
   Or of yon starry clime—
An inmate of the ocean graves,
   Or of the heavens sublime?
Is thy mysterious place of rest
The eternal mansions of the blest,
   Or the dim shores of time?

Hast thou forever won
   A high and glorious name,
And proudly grasped and girdled on
   The panoply of fame—
Or wanderest thou on weary wing,
A lonely and a nameless thing,
   Unchangingly the same?

Thou answerest not. The seal'd
   And hidden things that lie
Beyond the grave, are unrevea'ld,
   Unseen by mortal eye—
Thy dreamy home is all unknown,
For spirits freed by death alone
   May win the viewless sky.

THE LABORER.

BY WILLIAM D. GALLAGHER.

Stand up—erect! Thou hast the form,
    And likeness of thy God!—who more?
A soul as dauntless 'mid the storm
Of daily life, a heart as warm
    And pure, as breast e'er wore.

What then?—Thou art as true a MAN
    As moves the human mass among;
As much a part of the Great Plan
That with Creation's dawn began,
    As any of the throng.

Who is thine enemy?—the high
    In station, or in wealth the chief?
The great, who coldly pass thee by,
With proud step, and averted eye?
    Nay! nurse not such belief.

If true unto thyself thou wast,
    What were the proud one's scorn to thee?
A feather, which thou mightest cast
Aside, as idly as the blast
    The light leaf from the tree.

No :—uncurb'd passions—low desires—
    Absence of noble self-respect—
Death, in the breast's consuming fires,
To that high nature which aspires
    Forever, till thus check'd:

These are thine enemies—thy worst;
    They chain thee to thy lowly lot—
Thy labor and thy life accurst.
Oh, stand erect! and from them burst!
    And longer suffer not!

Thou art thyself thine enemy!
    The great!—what better they than thou?
As theirs, is not thy will as free?
Has God with equal favors thee
    Neglected to endow?

True, wealth thou hast not: 't is but dust!
    Nor place: uncertain as the wind!
But that thou hast, which, with thy crust
And water, may despise the lust
    Of both—a noble mind.

With this, and passions under ban,
    True faith, and holy trust in God,
Thou art the peer of any man.
Look up, then—that thy little span
    Of life, may be well trod!

LINES ON GREECE:

RECITED IN THE CINCINNATI THEATRE, FEBRUARY, 20TH, 1824, AT A THESPIAN PERFORMANCE FOR THE BENEFIT OF THE GREEKS.

BY PEYTON S. SYMMES.

WHEN lowly Merit feels misfortune's blow,
And seeks relief from penury and wo,
How thrills with rapture every generous heart,
To share its treasures, and its hopes impart,—
As, rising o'er the sordid lust of gold,
It shows the impress of a heavenly mould!

And, if a single sufferer thus may find
Each eye o'erflowing, and each bosom kind,
How should we feel when *Nations* rend the air
With blended shouts of victory, and despair!
How feel, when glorious GREECE *herself* appears,
Sublime o'er ruins of a thousand years,—
Recites the harrowing story of her woes,
Since first the Turkish crescent o'er her rose,—
And asks of free AMERICA, the aid
Which lies in *every* Freeman's *heart* and *blade!*

Such is the land which now contends alone,
In proud defiance of a ruffian's throne;—

Beneath whose sway for centuries she bore
The wrongs and suff'rings *she shall feel no more!*

The long, the cheerless night of Slavery's reign
At last is o'er,—and Freedom smiles again:
Smiles to behold how all-defacing Time
Has swept in vain o'er that delightful clime,
Nor yet subdued the spirit which of yore
Shed glory's halo round her classic shore.
What though her towers are fall'n, her arts decayed,
Not Time alone the mournful change hath made;—
'T was Slavery's mildew-breath, and Rapine's sway,
That tore her sculptured monuments away,—
Till, ev'n within Minerva's sacred Dome,
The Mosque has found a desolated home!

And shall Columbia's rulers coldly stand,
With listless gaze, and unextended hand,
Till Greece, regenerate, shall her freedom find,
Or firmer fetters Tyranny rebind?
Must Greece, the inspiring theme of bard and sage,
The pride of every lettered clime and age,—
Surrounded by her impious foemen, strive
To keep the hallowed flame of hope alive,
Without one friendly arm the sword to wield,
In Freedom's cause, on Glory's battle field?—
Forbid it, Heaven!—or be the tale unknown
That 't was not *thus* our Sires achieved *their own!*

In vain her poets sung, her heroes fought,
In vain her Sage enlarged the bounds of thought,
And, vainly, matchless Phidias toiled for fame,—
Should now a thankless world *deny* the claim!
—And yet, when in our councils lately rose
The voice of sympathy for Grecian woes,
The noblest efforts of her champions failed,
And cold mistrust o'er eloquence prevailed.

Yet still—although COLUMBIA may not send
Her Fleet, the cause of Freedom to defend,
Lest Allied jealousy the act should view
As fraught with danger to the kingly crew;
—Though by our Statesmen it is deemed unsafe
The angry Lions in their lair to chafe,
Lest we should rouse them to a nimbler leap,
O'er the rude surges of 'the vasty deep,'
And find too late—by savage force o'erpowered—
We are not ev'n 'the *last* to be devoured;'
—Though neither Turkish faith, nor moslem laws,
Must be invaded in that *holiest* cause,
Which aims to rescue from enthralling chains
Heroic millions, in whose fervid veins
The swelling current of the patriot flows,
And in whose hearts the Spartan's ardour glows:
—Though *nothing*, now, our COUNTRY dares to give
To her who nobly *scorns* in *chains* to live!—
Still may each kindred spirit *plead* her cause,
Nor wait the lingering sanction of our laws;—

Still may our Thespian band the tribute pay,
That from the ruthless spoiler rends his prey;
And waft to that loved land the Drama's aid,
Amid whose groves the young THALIA strayed,
And all the tuneful Nine their earliest powers displayed.

Nor shall the boon be lost;—though small the sum,
'T will nerve the Grecian's arm, when perils come,
To know a Christian People's prayers arise,
With hope-inspiring ardor, to the skies,—
That heaven's Almighty arm may interpose,
And GREECE be rescued from her DIREST FOES.

ARNOLD OF WILKENREID.*

BY JAMES H. PERKINS.

CAN ye be slaves? (and as he spoke,
His proud lip curled, and from his eye
The light of conscious triumph broke,)
Will ye be slaves, when ye can die?—
The mountains that our Maker gave
To be our home, are bald and steep,

---

* Supposed to be spoken by Arnold of Switzerland, who, in a battle with the Austrians, suffered himself to be trodden to death by his own countrymen, while by grasping and directing against himself a number of the Austrian spears, he opened a passage into their phalanx, otherwise impenetrable.

But there is room there for a grave;
The curling mist, and drifting cloud—
Are they too cold to be a warrior's shroud?
No. To that land our hearts are knit;
There do our loved ones' ashes sleep;
And floating on the midnight air,
Around each grassy hillock there,
The spirits of our fathers flit.
Their feet the rugged mountains trod,
Nor asked they that man's leave be given;
Their fetter was the will of God,
Their dungeon was the dome of heaven.
Let us none other know;
Brethren, myself a sacrifice
I offer to the foe.
If you have loved yon land—
If you have loved the young, the fair,
That you have left to tremble there,
While with your own right hand,
Your own heart's blood, you win for them a home;
If you have loved to hear
The carol of the mountaineer,
—Whose birthright 't is to roam,—
Come swelling loud, and long, and clear,
Upon the morning air;
If you would scorn to wear
The fetters of an earthly lord,
Unknown, accurséd, and abhorr'd;

If, when these hills, around us now,
'Mid fervent lightnings pass away,
And darkness veils yon sun,—
Within the halls of living day,
Before the never-dying One,
Ye would stand forth with dauntless brow,—
Come now with me; and when the breath
Is trodden from this iron frame,
And all this strength is lost in death,
Then be your battle-cry, my name.
And if ye win this day;
If Switzerland again is free—
When, gathered by the mountain tree,
Ye tell men of this fray,
And fight your battle once again,
Numbering o'er the martyred slain,—
May I not hope that I shall share
The burning tear, and whispered prayer?
But if ye win it not;
If Austria's tyrant shall have power,
To make ye mourn this day, and hour,
And all accurs'd this spot;
If you must live as slaves, or flee,
Weep if you will—for liberty;
Weep for the country of your birth;
Weep for yourselves, your race, the earth,
But not a tear for me.

THE PATHS OF LIFE.

AN ADDRESS TO A CLASS OF GIRLS, ABOUT LEAVING SCHOOL, IN INDIANA.

BY MRS. LAURA M. THURSTON.

Go FORTH—the world is very wide,
   And many paths before ye lie,
Devious, and dang'rous, and untried;
   Go forth with wary eye!
Go! with the heart by grief unbow'd!
Go! ere a shadow or a cloud
   Hath dimm'd the laughing sky!
But, lest your wand'ring footsteps stray,
Choose ye the straight, the narrow way.

Go forth—the world is very fair,
   Through the dim distance as ye gaze;
And mark, in long perspective, there,
   The scenes of coming days.
Orbs of bright radiance gem the sky,
And fields of glorious beauty lie
   Beneath their orient rays;
Yet, ere their altered light grow dim,
Seek ye the Star of Bethlehem!

Go forth—within your distant homes
   There are fond hearts that mourn your stay ;
There are sweet voices bid ye come ;
   Go—ye must hence—away !
No more within the woodland bowers
Your hands may wreathe the summer flowers,
   No more your footsteps stray ;
To hail the hearth, and grove and glen,
Oh, when will ye return again !

Not when the summer leaves shall fade,
   As now they fade from shrub and tree,
When autumn winds, through grove and glade,
   Make mournful melody ;
The long, bright, silent autumn days,
The sunset, with its glorious blaze,
   These shall return—but ye——
Though time may all beside restore,
Ye may come back to us *no more*.

Go—ye have dreamed a fairy dream,
   Of cloudless skies and fadeless flowers,
Of days, whose sunny lapse shall seem
   A fete 'mid festal bowers !
But of the change, the fear, the strife,
The gathering clouds, the storms of life,
   The blight of autumn showers,
Ye have no vision—these must be
Unveiled by stern reality !

Ye yet must wake (for time and care
  Have ever wandered side by side,)
To find earth false, as well as fair,
  And weary too, as wide.
Ye yet must wake, to find the glow
Hath faded from the things below,
  The glory and the pride!
To bind the willow on the brow,
Wreathed with the laurel garland now.

But wherefore shall I break the spell
  That makes the future seem so bright?
Why to the young glad spirit tell
  Of withering and blight?
'T were better: when the meteor dies,
A steadier, holier light shall rise,
  Cheering the gloomy night:
A light, when others fade away,
Still shining on to perfect day.

Go then—and when no more are seen,
  The faces that ye now behold—
When years, long years shall intervene,
  Sadly and darkly told—
When time, with stealthy hand, shall trace
His mystic lines on every face,
  Oh, may his touch unfold
The promise of that better part,
The unfading spring-time of the heart!

THE BLIND GIRL.

BY MRS. AMELIA B. WELBY.

I sit beneath the grape-vine that o'ercreepeth
   The humble arch above our cottage door,
While on its purple clusters softly sleepeth
   The holy radiance that the moonbeams pour;
The joyous song-bird in the starlight singeth
   Unto the dreaming birds its vesper hymn,
But not a single ray of gladness springeth
   Within my heart—alas! my eye is dim.

I know the hour when silent-footed Even
   Puts on her shadowy mantle, light and fair,
When, as she waves her wand o'er earth and heaven,
   The stars float up within the soft blue air;
'T is then I fling aside my long loose tresses,
   Unto the kisses of the wanton wind,
And strive to sing and pray—but ah! there presses
   A gloomy pall upon me—I am blind!

Oh! could I steal forth, when the daylight fadeth
   From rock and tree, to greet the summer eves,
To watch the primrose that from sunlight shadeth
   Its golden cup, unfold its twilight leaves;

To lay my warm brow to the breeze that wooeth
   The wild sea-ripples to the sounding shore,
The soft south breeze that perfume round us streweth:
   But, ah! 't is vain, my eye is shaded o'er.

My little sister often softly layeth
   Her velvet cheeks to mine, and bids me go
Where the young moss-rose its soft bloom displayeth,
   And the wild daises in their brightness glow;
I hear her small feet as she lightly dances,
   Like a wing'd fairy o'er the emerald grass—
She thinks not of her sister's clouded glances,
   For where she trips the blind girl may not pass.

When my young brother in his beauty boundeth
   Up with the lark to greet the morning sky,
While through the forest-aisles his laugh resoundeth,
   The tear drops gather in my darken'd eye;
And when, with rosy cheek and bright eye burning,
   He seeks my side in all his boyish glee,
My heart is troubled with a secret yearning
   To meet his glance—but, ah! I cannot see.

My meek fond mother tells me I am brighter
   Than the bright flowers she twines amid my hair,
She thinks her praise will make my spirit lighter,
   But, oh! I pine not to be bright or fair;
I may be lovelier than the violet flower,
   That shines, they say, beneath its broad leaves hid;

But beauty is to me a worthless dower,
  While darkly rolls my eye beneath its lid.

I cannot gaze upon their pleasant faces,
  Where the soft light of beauty ever beams,
Yet on my mind their fair forms Fancy traces,
  And their deep looks pierce through my nightly dreams.
I feel my mother's soft eye as it flashes
  Like a lone star that looks down from the sky,
Trembling so lightly 'neath its silky lashes—
  Yet when I wake 't is with a darken'd eye.

Ah! little know they of the dreamy sadness
  That shadows o'er my spirit's viewless urn,
For they can look out on the free world's gladness,
  Where blossoms blow and stars shoot out and burn,
While I must sit a fair, yet darken'd flower,
  Amid the bright band gather'd round our hearth,
The only sad thing in our bright home bower.—
  Oh! for one glance upon the fresh green earth!

HISTORY.

BY WILLIAM NEWTON.

Life has two realms: the fanciful and true.
The first is infinite—but yet has bounds;
The last is bounded—but is unconfined.
The ministers of fancy, are the vast
And deathless elements of Nature. They
Exist within us, and around us; and
Control our very being. They impart
A portion of their nature to our thoughts—
They sway us with imaginary hopes—
They force us from our purpose: and assume
The form of our desires, yet keep us back
From their attainment, when we crave it most.
They own no form, but take each one by turns,
That thought or nature furnishes. They seem
But phantoms of reality; yet are
The very tyrants of our freest thoughts.
Reality has greater power: it gives
A form and substance to our wildest dreams.
It far exceeds them; for what power can bound
The movements of the mind? When hope or hate,
Love or ambition, reason, pride, revenge,
Rouse it to action, *who* can rule the storm?

I had a vision in my waking hours;
And in its course, the order of all time
Went by before me. Nature was unchanged;
But the bright sunlight of the mind was gone:—
That mighty principle which sways its power
As the moon sways the ocean, was extinct.
Ambition saw its loftiest hopes give way,
And topple to the tomb: and men looked on
As Fame's last sunbeam faded from the sky,
And left the memory of their noblest deeds
As trophies for *Oblivion*, who held
The sceptre of unlimited control.
The ocean of the mind was waveless now:—
Passion and intellect, like winds at rest,
Failed to arouse it,—they had lost their power.
Time passed away; and every age described
The circle of man's destiny. The past
Brought with it no instruction: its broad page
Bore but *one* name,—and that, *Forgetfulness.*—
It was a spell-word on the intellect—
It was the South-wind * to the poet's harp,
And silenced all its music. Men beheld
The landmarks of the intellect thrown down.
Genius and folly held an equal rank,
And met the same reward,—a nameless end.
Motive had lost its power; its very name
Became a mystery, and seemed to speak,

* ' This wind (the samoor) so softens the strings of the lutes, that they can never be tuned while it lasts.'

Like a sad relic, of departed times,
Which had no date in human memory.

  I looked again ; and saw a being rise,
Like a new Venice, from the wave of time.
There was a majesty about her brow,
That told of lofty thoughts ; and, in her eye,
A power to pierce through the remotest times.
She ruled the past—but to the future gave
The lessons of her wisdom ; and her gifts
Became the heirlooms of humanity.
Her power was boundless. Nature was her field,
And Time her minister. E'en Death resigned
A portion of his ministry, and claimed
No power o'er those, where HISTORY set her seal.
She gave the shadowy beings of the past
A name and an existence, and their deeds
Became the oracles of future time.
She wrote the patriot's name on the same scroll
Where she inscribed the traitor's ; and to both
  She gave the same reward. What could she else ?
She makes a name immortal. Its *regard*
Is the just consequence of its *desert.*
The gift which is an Arnold's curse, becomes
A Washington's best blessing ; since it sends
The memory of their deeds through every age.
Nor was Oblivion powerless ; for the dread
Of meeting, like the brute, a nameless end—
Of perishing, without a record left

To tell of lofty thoughts, or noble deeds,
Roused every power, and drew to its full bent
Each thought and purpose. Intellect awoke
And won its loftiest honors. Genius saw
The kingdom of the universe unfold
Its richest treasures ; and it took from thence
The gems of brilliant and undying thought.
The wish to be remembered ruled each mind,
And swayed each motive. Virtue, vice, or power,
Were each employed, as ministers of fame.
Some, by great actions made themselves a name ;
And some, by blasting greatness. There were minds
So dwarfish in the stature, as to fall
Beneath the horizon of the common mass,
Yet, rising on the pyramid of vice,
They stood exposed, in open infamy ;
Heirs of man's scorn, and time's relentless curse !

BIRTH-DAY OF WASHINGTON.

BY GEORGE D. PRENTICE.

Why swell a million hearts as one
  With memories of the past?
Why rings out yon deep thunder gun
  Upon the rushing blast?
Why hold the beautiful and brave
  The jubilee of earth?
It is, it is the day that gave
  Our patriot hero birth.

We offer here a sacrifice
  Of hearts to him who came
To guard young Freedom's paradise
  With sword of living flame!
To him who in War's whirlwind loud
  Rode like an angel form,
And set his glory on the cloud,
  A halo of the storm.

A hundred years, with all their trains
  Of shadow, have gone by,
And yet his glorious name remains
  A sound that cannot die!

'T is graven on the hill, the vale,
    And on the mountain tall,
And speaks in every sounding gale
    And roaring water-fall!

No marble on his resting spot
    Its sculptured column rears,
But his is still a nobler lot—
    A grateful nation's tears.
Old Time, that bids the marble bow,
    Makes green each laurel leaf
That blooms upon the sainted brow
    Of our immortal chief!

His deeds were ours—but through the world
    That mighty name will be,
Where glory's banner is unfurl'd,
    The watchword of the Free;
And as they bend their eagle eyes
    On Victory's burning sun,
Their shouts will echo to the skies,
    "Our God and Washington!"

'TIS SAID THAT ABSENCE CONQUERS LOVE.

BY FREDERICK W. THOMAS.

'T is said that absence conquers love!
   But, oh! believe it not;
I 've tried, alas! its pow'r to prove,
   But thou art not forgot.
Lady, though fate has bid us part,
   Yet still thou art as dear—
As fixed in this devoted heart,
   As when I clasp'd thee here.

I plunge into the busy crowd,
   And smile to hear thy name;
And yet, as if I thought aloud,
   They know me still the same;
And when the wine-cup passes round,
   I toast some other fair;—
But when I ask my heart the sound,
   Thy name is echoed there.

And when some other name I learn,
   And try to whisper love,
Still will my heart to thee return,
   Like the returning dove.

In vain! I never can forget,
   And would not be forgot;
For I must bear the same regret,
   Whate'er may be my lot.

E'en as the wounded bird will seek
   Its favorite bower to die,
So, lady! I would hear thee speak,
   And yield my parting sigh.
'T is said that absence conquers love!
   But, oh! believe it not;
I've tried, alas! its power to prove,
   But thou art not forgot.

PARLEZ BAS.

BY JAMES G. DRAKE.

Parlez bas! The moon is up,
   And o'er the sleepy throng
The mocking-bird's high notes are heard,
   In wild and witching song—
No eye shall trace thy footsteps here,
But fear thee not while love is near.

Parlez bas! Though here we meet
    In silence deep, alone,
No guilty thoughts disturb our souls,
    Nor wish we fear to own.
Pure as the light yon orb imparts,
Shall be the meeting of our hearts.

Parlez bas! A genial breath
    Is wandering o'er earth's flowers;
Their fragrance mingles with thy voice,
    And holy joy is ours.
Parlez bas! and let each tone
Echo the fondness of mine own.

Parlez bas! And now repeat
    The vow those lips once made;
Mine is a love that cannot change,
    A heart that ne'er betrayed.
O say that thou wilt love me still,
Through storm or sunshine, good or ill.

Parlez bas! I bless thy words,
    The last that I may hear;
Sweet on my brow thy breath I feel,
    Upon my cheek thy tear.
Now take thee to thy bed and rest,
And be thou blest as I am blest.

SONG.

BY JAMES H. PERKINS.

Oh! merry, merry be the day,
 And bright the star of even—
For 't is our duty to be gay,
And tread in holy joy our way;
 Grief never came from Heaven,
   My love—
It never came from Heaven.

Then let us not, though woes betide,
 Complain of Fortune's spite, love;
As rock-encircled trees combine,
And nearer grow, and closer twine,
 So let our hearts unite,
   My love—
So let our hearts unite.

And though the circle here be small
 Of heartily approved ones,
There is a home beyond the skies,
Where vice shall sink and virtue rise,
 Till all become the loved ones,
   Love—
Till all become the loved ones.

Then let your eye be laughing still,
    And cloudless be your brow;
For in that better world above,
Oh! many myriads shall we love
    As one another now,
           My love—
As one another now.

OLDEN MEMORIES.

BY WILLIAM D. GALLAGHER.

There 's a voice from every bird,
There 's a tone in every tree,
That recalls some burning word
I have uttered when with thee:
There 's an eye in every star,
There 's a look in every cloud,
That bears my thoughts afar
Where thou rulest Fashion's crowd.

Every sweet and breathing flow'r
That scents the twilight breeze,
Hath a ministry and pow'r
Over " Olden Memories :"

Every ripple of the stream
That goes singing on its way,
Hath a tale of boyhood's dream,
And of manhood's merry May.

I have treasured every look,
I have garnered every tone,
Till my heart is like a book
Fill'd with memories alone:
I have asked no higher bliss,
'Mid the world's incessant din,
Since our last hope died, than this—
To *dream* of what hath been.

And in the silence of the night,
And 'mid the bustle of the day,
Oft a vision glads my sight,
And I wish it not away:
But I wonder then if thou,
In thy far and wedded home,
Ever think'st of him who now
To thy presence may not come.

THE END.